REIMAGINING NATIONAL BELONGING

Reimagining National Belonging

Post–Civil War El Salvador in a Global Context

R‍OBIN M‍ARIA D‍E‍L‍UGAN

THE UNIVERSITY OF
ARIZONA PRESS

Tucson

The University of Arizona Press
© 2012 The Arizona Board of Regents
All rights reserved
First issued as a paperback edition 2013

www.uapress.arizona.edu

Library of Congress Cataloging-in-Publication Data

DeLugan, Robin Maria.
  Reimagining national belonging : post-civil war El Salvador in a global context /
Robin Maria DeLugan.
      p. cm.
  Includes bibliographical references and index.
  ISBN 978-0-8165-0939-3 (cloth : alk. paper)
  ISBN 978-0-8165-3101-1 (paperback : alk. paper)
1. El Salvador—Politics and government—1992– 2. El Salvador—Social
conditions—20th century. 3. El Salvador—Social conditions—21st century.
4. Civil war—Political aspects—El Salvador—History. 5. Civil war—Social
aspects—El Salvador—History. 6. Political culture—El Salvador—History.
7. Nationalism—El Salvador—History. 8. Collective memory—El Salvador—
History. I. Title.
  F1488.5.D45 2012
  972.8405'2—dc23
                                                        2012013871

Manufactured in the United States of America on acid-free, archival-quality paper
and processed chlorine free.

17   16   15   14   13   6   5   4   3   2

Contents

Acknowledgments

This book is years in the making. It is the product of many visits to El Salvador. I gratefully acknowledge financial support from the Fulbright IIE, Social Science Research Council, Ford Foundation, and the University of California President's Postdoctoral Fellowship Program.

My years of research in El Salvador offer me the privilege of having strong relationships with many key people there. This research would not be the same without the participation of these valiant citizens who shared their concern about El Salvador and who see attention to questions of culture, history, and nation paramount to advancing society's well-being. It is not possible to name everyone in El Salvador who contributed to this research over the years. Special gratitude, however, goes to Consuelo Roque, Carlos Gregorio Lopez-Bernal, Carlos Lara Martínez, Gregorio Bello Suazo, Ramon Rivas, Georgina Hernandez-Rivas, Carlos Henríquez Consalvi, Rita Araujo, Santos Zetino, Juliana Ama de Chile, Fidel Flores, Miguel Angel Amaya, and Daniel Flores y Ascencio. The family Bonilla always provided a home away from home and I thank Roxana, Manuel, and Paulette for their big hearts and unwavering support. The Barahona family offered precious support, and I especially thank Don Luis Alonso, Tatiana, Eduardo, Valerie, Jonathan, and young Eduardo. Mil gracias to Monica Barahona. Visits to Tio Santiago in San Sebastian were always full of poetry and grace. During the writing of this book we lost Maria Melendez de Barahona, respected mother and grandmother. I cherish her memory.

Among the colleagues in the United States who have supported this journey and who have influenced my thinking, I recognize foremost my mentors Nelson Graburn and Rosemary Joyce. Aihwa Ong and Beatriz Manz guided the early stages of this project. I am thankful for Yuko Okubo, Kathryn Mathers, Amy Lonetree, Krisjon Olson, Renata Marsden, Beverly Davenport, Jessica Theissen, Nancy Postero, Mariane Ferme, Ellen Moodie, Brandt Peterson, Ana Maria Alonso, Jeffrey Gould, Aldo Lauria Santiago, Jonathan Fox, Erik Ching, Beatriz Cortez, Douglas Carranza, Susan Bibler Coutin, and Cecilia Rivas. Colleagues at the University of California, Merced, who have been generous with time and attention include Simón Weffer, Cristián Ricci, Ignacio Lopez-Calvo, Manuel Martin-Rodriguez, Virginia Adan-Lifante, Paul Almeida, Kathleen Hull, Linda-Anne Rebhun, and Jan Goggans. A 2010 book workshop at the University of California, Santa Barbara, provided valuable feedback that helped me to polish my final manuscript. I thank George Lipsitz, Clyde Woods (rest in peace), Douglas Daniels, Esther Lezra, Claudine Michel, Felice Blake, Tomas Avila-Carrasco, Heidi Hoechst, Steven Osuna, Jonathan Gomez, Alison Jefferson, Jordan Camp, Christine Heatherton, and Ingrid Banks for their generosity of time and excellent feedback. My fellow board members of Three Nations Indian Circle sustained me along this journey, and I thank Guillermo Vasquez, David Escobar, Roberto Alfaro, Vanessa Yava, Concha Saucedo, Lorena Montoya, and Atzintli Mazatl. Two anonymous reviewers provided valuable feedback that made the book stronger. Don Myers performed quality control by reviewing the final manuscript. I praise his scrupulous attention to detail and his dedication to helping me tell this story in a clear style that I hope will attract many readers.

Finally, I could not have completed this book without the love and support of my family, Sebastian Barahona, Reynaldo Barahona, Natalia Barahona, Nancy DeLugan, Linda Moriarty, Rande White and family, Loretta de Porceri, Michele Myers, Phoebe Ackley, Carmen Foghorn, Dixie Padello, Olga Stornaiuolo, Maria Zandstra, Alice Goss, Jim Goss, Rosalea King, and others who know that although they are not mentioned by name, they are no less appreciated. I thank them for motivating me to succeed.

Reimagining National Belonging

Introduction

Nation Out of War

HOW ANY NATION-STATE recovers from civil war is a topic of vital interest and importance to the contemporary world. From the formal political arrangements and institutional reforms that return a society to peace, to the reconstruction of social ties, postconflict nation-building involves many actors and processes. This book is a study of how El Salvador emerged from a twelve-year civil war (1980–1992) and grappled with this monumental task. By examining a series of simultaneous strategies for redefining the meaning of national belonging in El Salvador, I explore how postwar nation-building is resulting in a more just and inclusive definition of national belonging. This ethnographic research presents many of the actors involved in the complex process of reimagining the nation, not only from the perspective of the aftermath of civil war, but also in its contemporary global context, wherein nation-building is not just an intimate project involving a national state and its citizens, but a project engaging international actors and responding to external factors and influences. My intention is not to record a single snapshot in time of El Salvador, but to allow the reader to follow along as I illustrate certain fundamental aspects of the ongoing project of nation-building.

El Salvador emerged from civil war just as the international Cold War was ending. The global transition transformed political boundaries as well as social worlds. For example, the former Soviet bloc fragmented into a multitude of independent nation-states. Then, as now, nation-building continued apace. In Africa, Sudan recently split into two nation-states, one in the north and one in the south. The ongoing plight of Israel and Palestine suggests that creating a Palestine nation-state may be necessary to resolve the current political strife. It remains to be seen if the democratization movements of the Arab Spring 2011 will re-make state and society relations that underpin national identities and nationalisms in the region. Whether nation-building accompanies new state and territory formations, or whether it is about the ongoing maintenance of existing nation-states, the process involves the consolidating of collective identity, accentuating uniqueness, and defining what it means to belong to the nation. It is my contention that the technologies and discourses of nation-building that this book describes for El Salvador, including the global context that influences these practices, are instructive for comparing other emerging and ongoing projects around the globe.

At the end of its brutal civil war, the government of El Salvador and key social actors within and outside the country were left with the challenge of mending the social fabric of this nation. There is a substantial body of new scholarship that explores the recent history of El Salvador from a variety of angles. My research is in conversation with a number of scholars writing from a variety of academic disciplines who examine postwar El Salvador through specific topics such as indigenous identity (Ching and Tilley 1998; B. Peterson 2006; Tilley 2005); social memory and history (Gould and Lauria-Santiago 2008; Lindo-Fuentes, Ching, and Lara Martínez 2007); migration and diaspora (Baker-Cristales 2004; Coutin 2007, 2010; Hayden 2003; Menjívar 2000; Pedersen 2004; Rivas 2007; Rodriguez 2005); postwar violence and gangs (Cruz 2007; Hume 2009; Moodie 2010; Wade 2003; Zilberg 2004, 2007); social movements and democracy including the struggle for health rights (Almeida 2008; Smith-Nonini 2010; Wade 2003; Wood 2003); and gender and revolutionary organizing (Silber 2011). A 2010 special issue of the journal *Urban Anthropology and Studies of Cultural Systems and World Development* featured new research on migrants from El Salvador and their diasporic and transnational ties. Thanks to this scholarly attention, a multifaceted view of contemporary Salvadoran state and society in a global context is now readily available. The present book, while complementing the scholarship listed above, fills a unique niche by documenting the sites, practices, and process of postwar nation-building.

The civil war had at least garnered worldwide attention, solidarity, and sympathy for the people of El Salvador. International actors, though, had also supported and prolonged the conflict, notably the US government, which gave financial support to the then-government of El Salvador and its military. Yet the international community also played a key role in the negotiations and peacemaking processes that finally ended the civil hostilities. In fact, it marked the first time that the United Nations (UN) sent peacekeeping troops to intervene in a nation's internal conflict by offering a police function. The tensions between local and international interventions in both the national conflict as well as postwar society raise important questions about the sovereignty of a nation-state in our global age.

Following the end of the civil war, the Salvadoran state made a concerted effort to reinvigorate a Salvadoran national identity and a sense of shared values and common purpose. In doing so the state had to contend with powerful contrasting forces, such as the legacies of the civil war that divided the national population and the prevalent trends of globalization and neoliberalism that exacerbated El Salvador's position of weakness in the world system. On one hand, globalization brought UN agencies and international norms into the postwar nation-building process. Universally accepted human values were promoted as fundamental to democratization and national stability, and new attention was focused on El Salvador's most vulnerable populations, in particular children, women, and indigenous ethnic minorities. On the other hand, globalization also influenced citizens' consumption practices, media options, tastes, cultural expressions, and more, creating tension with state efforts to promote the notion that Salvadorans shared a unique local cultural identity. Postwar El Salvador has seen an explosion of "hyper" (*hiper*) or high-end shopping stores and malls that feature globally circulating brands and products.[1] These malls have become preferred leisure-time destinations, even while the price tags make purchase out of the question for most Salvadorans. Other globalizing processes include the patterns of out-migration that began during the civil war and that have steadily accelerated. Today, in a nation with a population of approximately six million, an estimated emigrant population of nearly one-third that number lives outside the national territory. The material and cultural products that faraway citizens send back to El Salvador have had a similar globalizing effect, and it is not unusual to see Salvadorans wearing T-shirts emblazoned with the names of US sports teams, colleges, hometown events and organizations, or corporate logos. As in other emigrant–sending countries on the periphery of the world system, the economic remittances of faraway citizens have sustained El Salvador's economy, and the postwar state has endeavored to strengthen the affective ties of *hermanos lejanos* (faraway brothers and sisters) to their original homeland, thereby redefining the meaning of national belonging and the scope of state practices in the process.

The post–civil war nation-state was also undermined by dominant US and allied governments' international policies of neoliberalism. These policies affected the national economy, forced the privatization and reduction of government services, and increased out-migration. Further, cultural dimensions of neoliberalism, with its emphasis on shaping the individual citizen's duties and responsibilities, made their way into new national educational curriculum reform. As neoliberalism and economic globalization eroded the basic conditions of survival, state efforts to promote ideas of national identity and belonging risked being received with cynicism or lack of confidence; and these influences continue to affect internal efforts to promote a distinctive Salvadoran national identity. El Salvador's nation-building amid increasing globalization invites important comparisons with similar challenges confronted by many other nation-states, including the complexities of belonging to a particular nation in our present era.

Between 1993 and 2011 I conducted extensive ethnographic fieldwork in El Salvador on the topic of postwar nation-building in a global context, beginning with summer fieldwork in 1993, followed by eight-month stays in 1996 and 2000, and a return visit as a Fulbright scholar in 2004, as well as briefer return visits in 2007, 2009, and 2011. Conducting longitudinal research permitted me to follow policy in the making as well as its implementation, reception, and criticism. My goal was to identify and understand a process whereby a number of state-led and civil society projects emerged to respond to the questions: Who are we as a nation? What is our shared culture and history? What does it mean to belong in El Salvador? This new focus on reimagining the post–civil war nation brought forth new government institutions, policies, and programs. Changes were made to the nation's school system to introduce cultural identity into the national curriculum. The first university programs in history and anthropology were created. New museums and monuments appeared as mechanisms that might influence social memory. Multiple, simultaneous state-led, and popular efforts were developed to shape shared meanings about the nation. Many classic nation-building techniques were at work in El Salvador, as schools, museums, census, media, and public events were used to generate shared ideas about national belonging.

In the interest of representing a common national identity, state projects promoted an ethnically and racially homogeneous national society based on the ideology of *mestizaje*, which emphasized the historical blending of indigenous and Spanish biological and cultural roots. Yet popular initiatives also pressed the state to recognize El Salvador's indigenous Nahuat, Lenca, Cacaopera, and Maya ethnic minorities, urging that efforts be taken to improve their peripheral status.[2] These movements highlighted the ways that national belonging is a contested and troubled arena, even when the state and its citizens have common goals of nation-building; and the process in which they emerged brought attention to historical and ongoing exclusions, in particular those based on race and ethnicity. As briefly mentioned above, some state-led projects expanded the definition of the nation in unexpected ways by including faraway and migrating citizens. These efforts to reimagine the nation occurred while global neoliberalism crippled El Salvador's labor economy and constrained its new democracy. My research shows how, in the aftermath of civil war, various creative efforts attempted to rebuild national ties and promote the idea of the nation. In particular, the research chronicles the challenges and complexities of how to accomplish this task with a fragile nation-state, especially when the bonds between state and society are historically weak. Through activities of various ministries, such as the Ministry of Education and its sub–Ministry of Culture (now elevated to the independent status of the Secretariat of Culture), the government of El Salvador responded to the internal and external challenges, with very specific techniques of nation-building and particular ideas of what a reimagined nation should look like. At times these government projects seemed to work at cross-purposes and were met with internal and public commentary and criticism. My research illustrates a process that reveals both the relationship between nation-building and globalization and the more intimate relationship between culture, history, memory, and the nation-state.

El Salvador's postwar reconstruction and nation-building reveal what may happen to state and society after a war has officially ended. The ways that a postwar national community is reimagined show how practices of nation-building respond to twenty-first-century global conditions and expectations, and how such reimaginings rely on a complex set of relationships between culture, memory, and indigeneity, mediated by postwar national policies and programs. El Salvador's mode of challenging official silences and forgetting in the postwar era also offers ways to explore how society urges the state to address exclusions and past episodes of state violence. In addition, the book shows that nationalism has become a transnational project, as faraway citizens become important to the nation and the international community inevitably influences the nation-building process. These dynamics caught my attention as I conducted my research on postwar nation-building in El Salvador. Unfolding events and activities did more than illustrate the idiosyncrasies of state and society in El Salvador. They provided a tool for understanding the conditions of twenty-first-century nation-building everywhere, where global entanglements influence internal nation-state dynamics in contrasting ways. On one hand, the international community aids the development of under-resourced nations, often with such strings attached as requiring the adherence to particular social, economic, or political policies. Further, international human rights norms can serve as a resource for bringing minority exclusion or subaltern claims forward for a nation-state to redress and to expand social inclusion within the nation. On the other hand, these same global processes pose challenges to the idea of the unique nation. With states and societies around the globe subject to similar influences, national societies today can appear to be more alike than not, due to common practices of economy, politics, culture, and consumption.

The tensions created during rebuilding by this global context can be further illustrated as follows. In El Salvador, as elsewhere, a positive relationship to the nation-state brings membership, citizenship rights, inclusion, and well-being. Being a minority, a migrant, or "other," however, ensures no such guarantees. To combat exclusion and marginalization within postwar El Salvador, international human rights laws and institutions influenced postwar nation-building by setting norms and by attempting to influence broader nation-state inclusion, especially for children, women, and indigenous people. Meanwhile, however, neoliberal economic policies threw the national society into flux. Food and fuel prices skyrocketed as new Central American free trade agreements brought regional imports to the market, which competed with national production. Government services shrank. Massive protests known as "white marches" took place in 2002–2003 against state efforts to privatize the public healthcare system. The massive out-migration that accompanied the turmoil of civil war increased throughout the immediate postwar years. The well-being of many families and the health of the national economy became dependent on the remittances of faraway citizens. The recent global economic crisis has impacted this economic flow. As migrants in the United States struggle for jobs, their chance for survival is exacerbated by stringent post–September 11 immigration policies and the latest wave of nativist alarm. Some migrants are unable to send support, some are forced to return to their homeland, and for others the prospect of migrating for a better life becomes less attractive. All of these factors influenced the reimagining of postwar national belonging.

Background: Emerging from Civil War

El Salvador's twelve years of civil war between popular revolutionary forces and the government's military were characterized by notorious acts of violence. Archbishop Monseñor Oscar Romero was assassinated in 1980 as he officiated at a public mass. The assassination occurred one day after Romero had delivered a homily calling upon the military to stop its repression and death squad massacres.[3] An international Truth Commission later revealed that Roberto D'Aubisson, founder and leader of the political party Alianza Republicana Nacionalista (ARENA), had ordered Romero's assassination. On December 11, 1981, in El Mozote, a remote village in the department of Morazan, 1,100 villagers (mostly children, women, and elderly men) were rounded up, brutally murdered, and dumped into mass graves (Binford 1996). Their deaths were a military tactic aimed at generating fear in citizens who might collaborate with the guerrillas. On November 16, 1989, a military battalion entered the Jesuit-administered Universidad Centroamericana "José Simeón Cañas" and murdered six Jesuit priests, including Segundo Montes, one of El Salvador's most prominent intellectuals. Two female co-workers at the Universidad Centroamericana were also killed. There were many other acts of military, paramilitary, and guerrilla violence. The 1993 Truth Commission Report to the United Nations established that the opposition group Farabundo Marti Liberación Nacional (FMLN)[4] was guilty of "grave acts of violence." However, it found the government's armed forces and allied groups culpable for the vast majority of abuses of human rights and humanitarian law. During the civil war an estimated 75,000 Salvadorans lost their lives, were tortured, or "disappeared." Meanwhile, tens of thousands fled the violence of the civil war and the pressures of a divided society. They left El Salvador, becoming refugees, going into exile, and settling primarily in the United States, but also in Canada, Australia, Europe, and elsewhere.

This civil conflict took place as the international Cold War antagonisms were winding down, yet many analysts explain El Salvador's war in relation to Cold War interests and ideologies. However, the underlying causes of El Salvador's conflicts run deep through the history of the modern nation-state. Oligarchical rule supported by military regimes, extreme poverty, social and economic marginalization, and the steady removal of lands from the control of rural populations have motivated popular unrest for more than two centuries. For example, antecedents to the recent civil conflict can be found in the numerous nineteenth- and twentieth-century indigenous rebellions (Tilley 2005) and in the 1932 uprisings that linked urban labor interests with the hardships experienced by rural (mostly indigenous) populations, and led to swift state-authorized violence against those rural populations. In 1932, over a period of weeks, a minimum of 10,000 and a maximum of 40,000 people were murdered, according to a range of estimates (T. Anderson 2001; Gould and Lauria-Santiago 2008). This infamous dark episode of El Salvador's history is referred to as *la Matanza* (the Slaughter). The Matanza and the civil war are the two episodes that tend to highlight the limited knowledge most scholars and the public have about El Salvador.

On January 16, 1992, in Mexico City, the signing of the Chapultepec Peace Accords by the government of El Salvador and the FMLN brought an official end to the twelve-plus years of civil conflict. Reaching the end of the civil war involved the participation of the international community and a protracted process of dialogue and negotiation. In 1987 Costa Rica's president Oscar Arias had proposed that a "global solution" be found for El Salvador. In April 1990, the Geneva Accords were forged by both sides of the conflict and specified their commitment to end the armed conflict via a political route; impel democratization of the nation; guarantee the strict respect of human rights; and reunify Salvadoran society. In July 1990, the UN created the Mission of United Nations Observers in El Salvador to supervise adherence to these accords. UN civilian personnel and peacekeeping forces entered El Salvador. By 1992 El Salvador had begun to adopt the institutional terms of the peace accords, which included a process to integrate the guerrilla opposition into a democratic political system. Many international governmental and nongovernmental agencies, for example, the European Union, United States Agency for International Development, and agencies of the United Nations, rewarded El Salvador's peace process by delivering technical aid and institutional support, and by financing a range of social and economic development projects in the early years following the war.

My first visit to El Salvador was in January 1992, immediately following the signing of the Peace Accords. I was there for a personal visit to introduce my one-year-old son to his Salvadoran grandparents and was not yet considering research possibilities. I still remember the exuberant celebrations. Although the nation was exhausted from war, most people seemed optimistic about the future. My attention was drawn to the unique opportunity offered by contemporary El Salvador to learn more about how an unfolding democratic transition could be accomplished, and how state projects would rebuild and redefine the nation.

The peace accords brought increasing democracy to El Salvador, in particular by legitimating the FMLN as a bona fide political party and thereby increasing political pluralism. During the course of the majority of my research, however, the ARENA party held the presidency, and its right-wing ideology dominated state policies. ARENA adopted neoliberal economic policies that were more in line with the conservative political party's commitment to free market ideology, and this contrasted with the FMLN's primary focus on the state's responsibility to develop policies and programs to address endemic social and economic problems and inequalities. While it would seem to be in the best interest of any political party in power to engage in postwar nation-building practices that aim to unify society around shared values and a common identity, I argue that national ideology can also distract citizens' attention from other state decisions and policies that do not equally benefit all citizens, for example, the ARENA government's adherence to neoliberal economic reform. This book is primarily focused on the state institutions of El Salvador, the practices and sites of representation, and the content of new meanings that appeared about the nation. I do not delve into the national party politics in any great detail, except to acknowledge certain challenges and contests to official efforts to instill and communicate ideas about national belonging. That said, it is important to note that in 2009, seventeen years after the signing of the peace accords that ended the civil war, the FMLN political party finally won the presidency.

I visited El Salvador in July 2009 just after the historic installation of Mauricio Funes as the new president. In March of that year El Salvador had elected Funes of the FMLN political party to lead the nation.[5] The election was noteworthy for a number of reasons, foremost because the FMLN had represented the guerrilla faction at the end of the civil war. Funes's election also marked the first time that El Salvador would be governed by a leftist political party. This occurred at a time when the FMLN also led municipal-level politics. The noteworthy election of Funes ended a long history of authoritarian government rule and ended national political domination by ARENA, a party that had held presidential power since 1989. Unfortunately, El Salvador's ongoing high levels of homicide and insecurity marred this dramatic and historic postelection democratic transition. It also occurred at a time when global neoliberal policies continued to erode nation-state autonomy and the national economy was faltering. While I conclude this book with suggestions about how state practices of nation-building are transforming under the new political leadership, this is an important topic that is continuously unfolding and remains to be studied further.

Studying Nation-States

The cultural turning point in the study of nation-states and projects of nation-building owes much to the work of Benedict Anderson. His principal thesis outlined in his book *Imagined Communities* ([1983] 2006) is that modern nation-building depends on the cultural practices of shared meaning-making that enable states and citizens to imagine themselves as co-members of a nation, including practices that foster fervent nationalism, feelings of alliance and allegiance, and a sense of common identity and belonging. Anderson traces the historical emergence of selected modern nation-states to highlight common processes that facilitate such a national imagination. Important to his thesis is the premise that, as membership in a unique nation is imagined, it is done concomitantly with attention to its co-existence within an international order. In anthropology and other related academic fields, the proliferation of studies of national culture and identity, cultural dimensions of globalization, and transnational belonging owe much inspiration to Anderson.[6]

Anderson's scholarship influenced the specific methods that guided the research for this book. My theorizing about the diverse processes of nation-building in postwar El Salvador builds on his ideas about nation-building as well as the ways that anthropology and other disciplines have both tackled and challenged his formative ideas. My primary focus is on governmental institutions and national cultural and educational policies and practices that emerged between 1992 and 2009 to promote official ideas about what it means to be from and belong to El Salvador. I highlight the role of a range of actors who participate as designers, contributors, critics, and audiences of the postwar projects. The actors in El Salvador include government officials, academics (in particular anthropologists and historians), intellectuals and opinion-makers, popular media, and indigenous leaders and organizations, as well as international actors such as representatives of UN agencies and individuals who represent Salvadoran emigrant and diasporic communities.

By focusing on state-led processes, this study is influenced by political anthropology and scholarship characterized as "ethnography of the state." We commonly refer to the central organizing government of a modern nation as "the state." However, we know that states are not isolated things-in-themselves. Though powerful as such, the state is more than a mere administrative apparatus for governance. The state binds all citizens within the process whereby the role and authority of the government to join a national territory and national population is legitimated, whether by consensus or coercion. Central to the historical processes are the constitutive role of culture and the relationship between culture and power that naturalize claims to governance and authority or that maintain a particular society's hegemony (cultural or otherwise). I have drawn inspiration from a number of case studies on historical state formation and transformation (Coronil 1997; Gledhill 2000; Hale 1994; Joseph 1994; Renan 1994 (1939 [1882]); Verdery 1996); on the role of the state in cultural nation-building (Alonso 1994; Anagnost 1997; Herzfeld 1986); exploring citizenship and governance (Ong 1996, 2003; Trouillot 1990); and states in the context of globalization (Borneman 1998; Trouillot 2000). A recent small boom in edited volumes evidences the growing interest in state-centered or state-engaged research in anthropology and related fields (Blom Hansen and Stepputat 2001; Coronil and Skurski 2005; Das and Poole 2004; Krohn-Hansen and Nustad, 2005; Nugent and Vincent 2004; Sharma and Gupta 2006; Steinmetz 1999).

While nations can exist without states, as in the example of ethnic or religious minorities that lack autonomous or centralized governmental authority or representation, states cannot exist without nations. It is, though, not automatic that individuals subjected to nation-state building go along with centralized projects to define the nation. Subjects may be ambivalent about their assigned status; disagree about enacted forms of governance or ideology; object to hegemonic representations of national culture and identity; or may be geographically distant or otherwise excluded from the state's efforts to administer to a national population. Nonetheless, nation-building and state-formation are linked processes. How a nation-state in the aftermath of civil war attempts to reconnect the members of its polarized society is also a study of the hyphen between nation and state.

This study of nation-building processes in the aftermath of civil war takes a holistic approach that is characteristic of anthropological research. Nation-building involves a variety of simultaneous multi-directional activities. While my focus is primarily on state-led sites and practices, I draw attention to the role of different social actors who also inform, support, and criticize official nation-building strategies. By reporting on simultaneous activities, I highlight a dialectic whereby various social actors and contemporary global conditions together exert influence on projects to define the nation and national belonging. This ethnography benefits from fieldwork stretching over a period of years as it allows me to comment on what has emerged and been transformed throughout the important developments that surround nation-building in postwar El Salvador.

State-Led Practices of Nation-Building

Following the civil war, the Salvadoran state, with the participation of local leaders, academics, intellectuals, popular media, international actors, and interested others, attempted to join together a divided postwar national society. This book focuses on their nation-building efforts by identifying who influenced and informed particular state-led projects, the content of postwar representations designed to shape ideas about national culture and belonging, and the official and nonofficial sites and practices that attempted to generate affinity with the nation. I understand nation-building as inevitably ongoing for all modern nation-states and not just for those emerging from conflict. In this study, however, I illustrate how, in the aftermath of civil war, the creative efforts by the state and interested others to shape shared meanings about the nation and belonging were in particularly sharp relief, especially as they represented early twenty-first-century contexts and concerns. This book focuses on the following key themes: the emphasis on culture in postwar national policies; a new meaning for indigeneity (the self and collective representation and recognition of indigenous identity) in nation-building that extends beyond mestizaje to include efforts to recognize El Salvador's contemporary indigenous population; how emigration makes nationalism a transnational project; and how social memory projects challenge the

nation not to forget past violence and atrocity. These themes are discussed below and represent the organization of the book.

Culture and Postwar National Policies

Chapter 1 examines how culture became an important focus in the
immediate aftermath of the civil war. In postwar El Salvador nation-
building practices focused on influencing attitudes, behaviors, and
shared meanings to create a sense of collective purpose and national
identity. Culture became the tool. The concept of culture was ap-
proached from various angles by El Salvador's state institutions.
Cultural identity was introduced into the national educational curriculum based in large part on the antecedent United Nations Educational, Scientific, and Cultural Organization (UNESCO) Culture
of Peace Program that was piloted in El Salvador. The program
looked to influence individual and collective behavior and attitudes
by teaching beneficent, universally accepted cultural values, such as
self-esteem, nonviolence, perseverance, and respect. Other attention
to national culture appeared via new university programs in anthropology, a new national museum of anthropology, a new government
secretariat of culture, and a proliferation of cultural museums. Chapter 1 examines how nation-building simultaneously engaged projects
that emphasized what was unique about Salvadoran culture and others that endeavored to instill a "universal" culture of peace.[7] Whether
presented as universally shared or particular, the emphasis on culture was central to the project of rebuilding the nation, and arguably
served as a useful tool (Yudice 2003).

A New Meaning for Indigeneity

In chapter 2 I describe how "the past" was a salient resource for
generating shared ideas about the nation and national belonging as
projects attempted to promote a sense of history and heritage. In
this direction, El Salvador followed similar nation-building practices commonly found historically and globally. These practices included the production of new official history textbooks. I show how

historians and other scholars, as social actors in the nation-building process, influenced new representations of the nation's past. Other actions, such as the 2004 inauguration of the Universidad de El Salvador's first academic program in history, underscored the new importance assigned to the study of the nation's past. At the same time, new history scholarship emerged to challenge certain official accounts about the nation's earlier periods, in particular the state's ongoing silences about state violence, war, and atrocity. State-led projects tended to avoid addressing troubling episodes in the recent past by focusing instead on a much deeper past.

Official projects that emphasized El Salvador's deep past primarily relied on archaeology to provide ancient symbols of unique cultural heritage and belonging. This level of attention to the national past involved the promotion of archaeological sites and displays of ancient material culture in celebration of El Salvador's indigenous roots. I observed these new promotions of national heritage being presented under an umbrella called "Maya" identity. In the ancient past, the region was likely a multiethnic frontier zone. We know that during the time of Spanish contact, Nahuat populations migrating from Central Mexico dominated the west, while Lenca and other groups influenced the east. Archaeological research continues to clarify Mesoamerica's complex cultural history. For post–civil war nation-building projects, however, "Maya" served as a useful metonym for indigenous cultures of the region. It served national tourism development by connecting El Salvador to the "Mundo Maya," a regional tourism and cultural history project. However, while state-led projects made indigeneity symbolically central to postwar meanings of the nation, contemporary indigenous populations continued to be kept socially peripheral.

Chapter 2 examines how nation-building processes that promoted El Salvador's deep past necessarily brought attention to the status of El Salvador's contemporary indigenous Nahuat, Lenca, Cacaopera, and Maya populations, which unofficial estimates suggest make up 10 percent of the national population. Over the decades El Salvador's national census has either undercounted or neglected to count at all its indigenous populations. The social, cultural, and political dynamics of race and ethnicity in El Salvador are complex. The majority population is of mixed Spanish and indigenous descent, and many markers of indigenous culture characterize El Salvador. Still, it can be difficult to identify who is an indigenous person on the basis of assumed markers of dress, language, or biological "purity." However, although ethnic cultural practices may not seem visible to the public, culturally vibrant indigenous communities do indeed exist in El Salvador, and over the years I have visited and established relationships with communities in both the eastern and western departments. This indigenous population of El Salvador is among the most impoverished and marginalized sectors of the national population. In chapter 2 I explore race, ethnicity, and nation in El Salvador by examining how postwar nation-building is gradually addressing the historical exclusion of indigenous populations.

Chapter 3 examines the exclusion of contemporary indigenous Nahuat, Cacaopera, Lenca, and Maya populations and other ethnic and racially diverse people in El Salvador. Various national allies and international entities and legal accords have supported contemporary indigenous populations, who challenged the state about their marginalization from national participation. Indigenous mobilizations increased in the immediate postwar period, and the government created a new Office of Indigenous Affairs. I discuss how state practices such as census technologies and UN reporting demonstrated the state's continued ambivalence toward indigenous ethnic minority populations, although signs of change were apparent as the state continued its ongoing effort to develop a *politica indígena* (indigenous policy). This chapter offers an examination of what it means to be indigenous in postwar El Salvador. I examine multiple approaches to indigeneity, emphasizing how indigeneity has become symbolically central to new ways of reimagining national belonging.

Nationalism as a Transnational Project

Chapter 4 examines specific state-led nation-building practices in El Salvador that responded to migration by reaching out to faraway citizens. There are few nation-states today that do not contend with migration, whether migrant-receiving or migrant-sending societies. The massive out-migration that occurred during El Salvador's civil war continues apace, and today there are an estimated two million Salvadorans living outside their national territory (mostly in the United

States). With El Salvador's national population totaling slightly more than six million, this represents a significant diasporic population. Members of the Salvadoran diaspora participate in El Salvador's economy through family remittances and in politics by lobbying from afar for favorite candidates, and they support Salvadoran society in myriad ways that reaffirm their ongoing connection and sense of belonging to the nation-state. I discuss the creation of the Ministry of Exterior Relations (Ministerio de Relaciones Exteriores), designed to address the Salvadoran populace abroad and to strengthen the affective ties of national belonging of diasporic citizens. I also show how popular media have contributed to state projects by connecting faraway Salvadorans to the nation-state. This chapter considers how the contributions of emigrant remittances, networks, and exchanges uniquely factor into the expansion of the meaning of national belonging that symbolically incorporates faraway citizens. I demonstrate how traditional nation-building technologies of the state such as the census and the map were uniquely reconfigured to include El Salvador's hermanos lejanos. While symbolic projects drew faraway citizens into the national imagination, in general those who migrated from El Salvador and the families they leave behind occupy the society's margins. There is a dark side of migration that has resulted in fractured families and the increase of gang violence and related social ills in El Salvador. Still, migration's major influence on state and society meant that my research on nation-building could not ignore its transnational dimensions. This chapter demonstrates, therefore, how nation-building today is also a transnational project as nation-states grapple with the impact of contemporary global conditions of migration and diaspora (Basch, Schiller, and Blanc 1994).

Social Memory Projects Challenge
Silences and Forgetting

The final chapter discusses the importance of national memory. I explore the relationship between museums, social memory, and nation. In San Salvador, the capital, there is a magnificent new national museum of anthropology. The new Museo Nacional de Antropología David J. Guzman is one of El Salvador's grandest buildings. It is monumental in size and importance. National museums are traditional institutions of nation-building. They ceremoniously legitimate official narratives of the nation's past, present, and future. That El Salvador's postwar government invested scarce resources to rebuild a more lavish version of its previous cultural history museum speaks to the importance accorded to culture and to the past by the postwar state. Chapter 5 walks the reader through the new museum of anthropology to explore the strategies employed to shape shared meanings about the nation. I link the new museum and its exhibitions to topics explored in earlier chapters in order to demonstrate how it grappled with ideas about national culture, explored how to represent the past, paid some attention to indigenous peoples' issues, and acknowledged the impact of international migration. I also discuss how this museum provided more than a source of static pedagogical exhibits by offering the public a unique and valuable social forum for a broad range of academic, cultural, and artistic activity.

In the postwar period there was a proliferation of new public nongovernmental museums that were also shaping national memory. The final chapter examines how museums and monuments undertaken by civil society initiatives supported state strategies to represent national belonging, but also tackled thorny issues by drawing attention to pivotal episodes of the nation's past and present about which the state remained silent. Universidad Tecnológica de El Salvador's elegant Museo Universitario de Antropología, Museo de Arte de El Salvador (MARTE), and the Museo de la Palabra y el Imagen (Museum of the Word and Image), all privately owned, yet public museums, tackled difficult topics such as the 1932 matanza and other indigenous peoples' issues, the violence of the civil war, and the human tragedy of contemporary migration.

Memory work conducted by public postwar museums and monuments is intimately connected to efforts to create a more just, equitable, and humane nation. Civil society was first to respond to recommendations in the 1993 Truth Commission Report to create a public memorial to the victims of war. The dramatic Monument to the Memory and the Truth was erected in San Salvador in December 2003 and is inscribed with the names of more than 25,000 victims of the civil war. This and other new sites, the result of public initiative, address topics that the state continues to avoid. The memory work inherent in these museums and monuments urged Salvadoran society to not let the violence and loss suffered by the nation escape public awareness or recede into oblivion. I present the memory work that emerged in El Salvador in connection with museums, monuments, and nation-building, I also index official silences.

Nation-Building as an Ongoing Project

El Salvador recently celebrated the twenty-year anniversary of the end of civil war. However, many grave social problems continue to plague the nation, and the social fabric remains tattered. The nation has one of the highest per capita rates of crime and violence in Latin America. Kidnapping, domestic violence, sexual abuse of children, and abandonment of newborn infants are regular occurrences. Gang activity that was all but unheard of when I started research for this project is now a widespread concern. The crime and violence can be understood as scars in the aftermath of the decade-long civil conflict of organized terror (Chavez 2004), but there are other possible explanations for the high rates of crime and violence. On one level, the violence can be associated with the state violence that enforced forms of social control for much of El Salvador's past. It is also indicative of the historically weak relationship between state and society. There is a fundamental lack of trust in the state and its commitment to serve Salvadoran society. As El Salvador appears to transition away from authoritarian modes of governance, it does so against a much longer history of state violence, impunity, and corruption that the public has come to expect. In addition, the local political-economic conditions that stratify society into a small wealthy segment and a massive poor population have not changed in any fundamental way.

It is important, therefore, not to equate the end of the civil conflict with the end of the deep divisions and structural inequalities that have long festered in the nation. Ellen Moodie's excellent 2010 ethnography about El Salvador looks at the nation from the opposite end of the telescope than does this book. While I focus on government policy and practices intended to strengthen national affinity, her research poignantly reminds us of the daily strife and violence that everyday Salvadorans, especially those on the margins of society, continue to endure. These troubling factors warp any social contract and contribute to continued crime and violence. In El Salvador "peace-time crimes and violence" occur on what Nancy Scheper-Hughes and Philippe Bourgois (2004) refer to as a "continuum of violence between war and peace." On this continuum, the misrecognition of symbolic and structural violence in both small and large acts serves to naturalize the conditions of violence (Bourdieu 1977). Thus, although post–civil war state-led projects attempt to shape meanings, values, and practices, structural factors can create unfavorable conditions that undermine the aims of the cultural nation-building projects. The alarming degree of social disintegration puts the fragile democracy of El Salvador at high risk. Public opinion polls indicating a concern about safety and security also show some support for a return of authoritarian government. Recent polls show that safety and security ranked higher than any other social or economic issue. Meanwhile, in search of solutions, the national government and interested social actors continue to focus on themes of national culture, history, memory, and belonging as a way to create national unity, collective identity, and shared culture and values. Throughout my fieldwork, I heard the questions: Who are we as a people? What is our history? What do we have in common? What is our vision for the future of our nation? In the answers to these questions are the meanings and practices that some hope will generate changes in popular attitudes, values, and deportment. The overall objective, therefore, of state-led and popular projects that focus on the nation is to cultivate a shared sense of nation-state commitment and belonging that will strengthen and stabilize postwar society, reduce fear and violence, and perhaps also permit the new democracy to grow.

1

Concentrating on Culture

Peace, Schooling, and Values

Education has to contribute to the national intention of forming a new citizen, more productive in the economic, more supportive in the social, and more participatory and tolerant in the political, more respectful of human rights and more peaceful in their relationship with their fellow beings . . . and for all of this, more proud to be Salvadoran.
—*Mario Fredy Hernandez, former president of El Salvador's Council of Higher Education. From his address at the UNESCO World Conference on Higher Education, October 5, 1998*

EL SALVADOR'S CIVIL WAR ended in January 1992. In the aftermath of war, state-led nation-building focused intently on culture as a mechanism for reconstructing national society. In El Salvador state-led practices addressed culture in two major ways: as an instrument that can transform the attitudes, thoughts, and behaviors of citizens, and as a vehicle for representing the nation's historical uniqueness and particularity (explored in detail in chapter 2). Both approaches relied on culture to construct shared meanings of national belonging, reduce social polarization, and alleviate postwar strife. From my interviews with people in government, academia, media, and so forth it was clear that the postwar emphasis on culture was new and innovative and influenced in part by a UNESCO pilot project to construct a "culture of peace" in El Salvador. This led to educational reform and cultural identity being introduced into the nation's curricula. The overture, one strategy to address civil strife and redefine national belonging, adopted a universal approach to shared culture and values. The historically specific context of the application and promotion of values and norms demonstrated the links between culture, society, and state power. It also highlighted the influence of the international community in the shaping of national society, reflecting the twenty-first-century global context of nation-building, and El Salvador's peripheral status therein.

This chapter discusses the emphasis on culture in El Salvador's postwar society. I start with efforts connected to the UNESCO Culture of Peace Program. The program offered a universal template based on selected principles and human values that are seemingly intended to be interchangeable from one postconflict nation-state to the next. I will argue that the Culture of Peace Program affected the behavior of the state as much as it attempted to affect citizens. I describe links between the UNESCO program and the goals of El Salvador's postwar government to form new citizens through national education. This chapter examines the changes made to the national educational system in 1998 that made cultural values central and focuses on schooling as a primary site and practice of nation-building. I pay attention to the role of the international community, as seen primarily through the UNESCO program, whose approach to democracy through emphasis on individualism matched the concurrent neoliberal tendencies in Western-dominated policies that had an effect on the decision-making of the postwar government and also strongly influenced El Salvador's culture-focused educational program. This chapter includes various critiques of the state's programs that focused on culture and values. I demonstrate not only how culture was important to postwar nation-building, but also the link between culture and power.

While "culture" is evoked as a tool of historical and contemporary nation-building, in anthropology the concept of culture has been the focus of much recent debate. While previous definitions encompass a holistic inventory of shared material culture, institutions, beliefs, traditions, and expressive culture, contemporary anthropologists challenge both the reification of culture and the evocation of timeless, primordial cultural expression (Abu-Lughod 1991). Today, in addition to focusing on the ongoing meaning-making and power-laden processes that generate culture, there is a critical lens on how culture is utilized in discourse and myriad political and economic strategies, pointing to what George Yudice refers to as the "expediency of culture" (2003). As the government of El Salvador and international actors aid postwar nation-building by turning to representations of national culture, it is with an instrumental goal of governance based on generating a sense of social cohesion, shared values, and collective identity. It is important to maintain a sharp analytical lens about the projects that unfold, as claims of eternal or primordial cultural ties are first and foremost meanings constructed in relation to the goals, interests, and needs of contemporary state and society.

From Culture of Peace to Global Governance

During years of fieldwork in El Salvador I traveled often by bus and sometimes by car throughout the nation, though most of my research was conducted in the capital, San Salvador. El Salvador's territory is small, and the capital is where centers of government, popular media production, most universities, and other cultural and artistic sites are concentrated. The sights and sounds of San Salvador are like so many Latin American capitals. Chugging diesel buses cough up black clouds while their ancillary personnel hang from bus entrances as they hawk the route, hustling yet more passengers into the often already over-crowded interiors. Once inside the bus, music blasts full-tilt with sounds ranging from Latin rhythms of salsa, merengue, and *cumbia* to the hip-hop and rock music of America's Top 40. The route hawking and radio-blasting of buses are matched by surrounding and competing horn honking (*pitos*) from bumper to bumper taxis, microbuses, and private automobiles that skillfully maneuver the perennially congested transportation arteries of El Salvador's largest city.

From the window of these moving vehicles, the sights and sounds of commerce abound. Street corners are filled with vendors (men, women, and young children) who work from makeshift venues to sell freshly peeled and pared mangos, papaya, and pineapple, or other foods standard to the local diet such as grilled cheese-filled *pupusas*.

Many women vendors gracefully balance wicker or plastic baskets (*guacales*) filled with produce on their heads. Mobile, these women weave between the cars that pause for red lights at busy intersections. With flashing smiles, they approach drivers and push the wares of the day. The characteristic lace-trimmed and multipocketed aprons worn by these women serve as flexible cash registers allowing for the completion of deft and rapid sales transactions. Local street vendors squeeze into public spaces that are increasingly overshadowed by global American fast-food chains of Burger King and Pizza Hut; tele-communications giants like Telecom; entertainment specialists such as Blockbuster; and by automobile lots that brim with popular (to the few who could afford them) imports such as Toyota and Peugeot.

From 1994 to 2009 I followed a number of simultaneously occur-ring state-led programs related to government goals of transforming a war-torn society by promoting ideas of national belonging. Field-work periods lasted as long as eight months while other visits were as short as a few weeks. Over time I became familiar with the ministries and agencies at the government center (*centro del gobierno*) and was able to identify and contact the social actors and cultural elites[1] who were actively involved with various postwar nation-building projects, whether contributing to and supporting state-led projects or critiqu-ing them. I observed key individuals as they imagined, implemented, evaluated, and criticized state-led strategies and practices. I also stud-ied postwar nation-building to examine the role of the international community. For El Salvador, a small nation with limited resources, international benefactors were necessary to remake the nation.

Benefactors in the guise of UN agencies or other supranational aid and development organizations, as well as national governments and agencies such as the United States Agency for International De-velopment (USAID), collectively offered a global template of sorts for how to rebuild postwar El Salvador. The macroeconomic reforms prescribed brought normative neoliberal relationships between state, society, and market to the democratizing society. In 2001 El Salvador exchanged its national monetary unit, the *colon*, for the US dollar, and in 2006 El Salvador was the first Central American nation to sign onto the Central American Free Trade Agreement. There was priva-tization of banking, telecommunications, electricity services, and pri-vate pensions. In addition to economic standards, El Salvador was guided in the ideals of liberal democracy, the role and responsibility of the state, and the participation of citizens. UNESCO chose El Salvador to pilot its Culture of Peace Program. At the program's core was the promotion of civic and cultural values deemed standard for democratic societies.

In the immediate postwar years, El Salvador received a tremendous influx of UN aid, technical support, and programs that attempted to model postconflict social development and democratization.[2] UNESCO's Culture of Peace Program was among those efforts. The program illustrates how projects to promote postwar culture and democracy extended beyond local state and society actors to include representatives and interests of the international community. It also offers an example of the attention to culture and education as tools for nation-building and governance in a neoliberal age. Irina Silber (2011) examines how in postwar El Salvador such democratic projects linked to neoliberalism emphasized empowerment and rights of citizenship; while at the same time these enforced structural adjustment programs disempowered and further impoverished Salvadorans. For further explanation she cites anthropologists Akhil Gupta and Aradhana Sharma: "Empowerment fits in with the neoliberal agenda of small government, participatory governance, and market based competitiveness. It enables developmentalist states to shift away from directly providing for the basic needs of their marginalized citizens to helping these citizens govern themselves and take care of their own development needs" (2006: 284).

As El Salvador terminated its civil war in 1992, UNESCO established the action Culture of Peace Program and selected El Salvador as one of three sites for its pilot test.[3] The Culture of Peace pilot program initially set out to inspire "cross-conflict participation in projects of human development" by emphasizing "superordinate goals," or goals that benefit all parties to the conflict (Lacayo-Parajon, Lourenco, and Adams 1996: 20).[4] Combining conflict management, social transformation, and human development, the stated objective was to achieve a higher "peace culture consciousness." Based on a vision of achieving peace and cooperation on a global scale, the Culture of Peace Program also acknowledged that such a universal goal would require a base of locally shared values, traditions, and culture. Initial decision-making about how to implement the Culture of Peace Program in El Salvador occurred in 1993 during the raw days of postwar peace. The process assembled representatives from UNESCO, the government of El Salvador, members of the FMLN (former guerrilla faction then transforming into a new political party), and local nongovernmental organizations.

The ability of the Culture of Peace Program to bring together a group of social actors polarized throughout the civil war was in itself a remarkable accomplishment. I interviewed individuals who participated in the early discussions. They characterized the group's interaction as marked by levels of aggression and mutual mistrust. Nonetheless, over a three-year period (1993–1996), they formed a working group that took as a starting thesis the idea that a focus on culture and cultural development would bring positive transformation and national reconciliation to Salvadoran society. The group was charged with developing a proposal for a number of short- and long-term projects for the Culture of Peace Program for El Salvador. The proposal was to address the following overarching objectives:

1. Contribute to the consolidation of the fulfillment of the peace process.
2. Contribute to social renovation in El Salvador, through the diffusion and individual and collective interiorization of the values, attitudes, and behaviors which are fundamental for peace.
3. Promote the process of learning and living a Culture of Peace that would not only transcend the simple transmission of knowledge, but also become the Salvadoran Society's form of day-to-day living.
4. Contribute to the international community an innovative experience in the construction of a Culture of Peace.[5]

The three-year period of intense cross-sector consensus-building and decision-making finally resulted in an elaborate proposal. It revolved around four project areas:

1. democratic citizenship and human development
2. recovery and development of national identity in a culture of peace
3. learning of and living a culture of peace

4. cross-cutting issues and projects, which basically referenced information systems and the training of personnel

For each project area there were specific justifications, objectives,
aims, target populations, and descriptions of projects and practices
for achieving the objectives. The defining characteristic in each project was an emphasis on formal and informal educational processes for
strengthening values to promote a peaceful and tolerant society and
to re-emphasize Salvadoran national identity. Here national identity
was used to describe the local, historical, traditional, and particular
dimensions of Salvadoran identity as opposed to other universal aspects of the peace project.

The budget for the comprehensive, multiyear proposal totaled
$32,782,000. The proposal was structured so that individual projects
could be pitched separately to potential donors as stand-alone projects. Among the stand-alone initiatives were projects to support El
Salvador's women, children, and indigenous communities (the signif-
icance of this latter emphasis will be discussed in upcoming chapters).
With proposal in hand, UNESCO representatives set out to locate
funding from international donors both for the holistic proposal and
for smaller, less costly piecemeal projects. Ultimately, however, they
were unable to finance more than a handful of projects.[6] Why was
this so? By 1996, four years had passed since the world's attention
was riveted on El Salvador's termination of the civil war. In my view,
by the time the Culture of Peace proposal was completed, most international sources of financial aid had moved on to other seemingly
more urgent priorities. Astri Suhrke and Julia Buckmaster (2005)
analyzed the patterns in international support for El Salvador. While
the pattern can be explained as an attempt to frontload aid instead of
spreading aid evenly over time, Suhrke and Buckmaster document
how insufficient funds were disbursed at the outset to achieve the
stated socioeconomic purposes. These patterns in funding might explain UNESCO's inability to identify major funding for the proposal.

Despite UNESCO's failure to secure funding for El Salvador's
elaborate Culture of Peace Program proposal, the years that the
working group toiled and the subsequent period wherein UNESCO
sought funding did have certain effects. Foremost, cross-sector social
actors overcame certain antagonisms and demonstrated they could

work together. This achievement alone drew much positive attention, and national newspapers regularly lauded the working group's
planning efforts. In addition, in 1998, six years after UNESCO's Culture of Peace Program was initiated, El Salvador's Ministry of Education (MINED) introduced a change in the national curricula that
mirrored the Culture of Peace proposal's emphasis on "Democratic
Citizenship and Human Development." The national education reform introduced the Program in Human, Ethical, and Civic Values
(Programa de los Valores Humanos, Eticos y Cívicos), hereinafter
the Values Program. Interviews with representatives in the Ministry
of Education stated that the objective of the curriculum reform was
"to create a culture of peace that contributes to the building of a
democratic society." They confirmed the connection between democratic citizenship and human development and the Values Program.
I discuss below the Values Program and how it addressed the state's
goal to use culture and schooling to create shared identity and to
form new citizens.[7]

The Values Program and Cultural Identity

Schools are social institutions well known for representing and re-
producing dominant ideas of the nation.[8] Classroom and schoolyard
training not only shape national collective identity, but also shape role
assignments within social structure pertaining to gender, economic
class, or ethnic minority status.[9] Schools can inform experiences of
national belonging in profound ways. In both the public and private
schools of El Salvador, uniform-wearing schoolchildren lined up each
day. With hand placed over heart they joined with fellow students,
teachers, and school staff in singing the national anthem . . . "Salu-
demos la Patria Orgullosas" (We Proudly Salute the Fatherland).
Through this daily school practice, students were trained in one of
the basics of citizenship, the ritual recognition of the nation-state.

As the words of Mario Fredy Hernandez that opened this chapter
illustrate, the government of El Salvador saw postwar nation-building
as an opportunity to form new citizens. Some of the strategies by
which the state attempted to achieve this goal were by relying on culture. In 1998 Cultural Identity (Identidad Cultural) was introduced

into the national curriculum and at its core was the Values Program. The national educational curricular reform offered a positive vision of society and attempted to cultivate shared values, collective identity, and attachment to the nation. It also introduced tools and techniques useful for the formation of national subjects and for further socializing citizens into expectations that inform commonsense understandings and everyday experiences. However, the Values Program's primary emphasis on the universal individual citizen (as opposed to focusing on the distinctive historical or social context or experience of being from El Salvador) also made the program and its goals appear transportable from nation to nation and therefore did not satisfy some educators and members of the public who wanted a program that placed more emphasis on El Salvador's unique culture and society. The state-led educational efforts to promote the Values Program were supported by national popular media, and media alliances revealed the mechanisms by which government-sponsored projects extended beyond the classroom to reach the broader Salvadoran public.

By the end of the civil war, El Salvador's educational system had fallen into shambles. Beginning immediately after the end of the war in 1991 discussions ensued about how to rebuild it. By June 1995, a systemwide educational reform proposal based on privatization and decentralization was put into action by then-president Armando Calderon Sol. Among the stated priorities in transforming the educational system was its role in the "moral and cultural reform of the Salvadoran society." A primary objective became how to shape perfect citizens (*cuidadanos cabales*) who would be conscious of their rights as well as their duties (Cardenal 2001: 349). Between 1995 and 2005 education reforms decentralized education; this was linked to the changed distribution of responsibilities between the state and the private sector in the delivery and/or financing of education services (Cuéllar-Marchelli 2003). Modernizing public administration was aimed at making it more cost effective for participants with the framework of a national decentralization and privatization strategy. The policy involved trade-offs and was not a panacea.

One of the first innovations by MINED was requiring the new curricular unit Cultural Identity in all schools, public and private, and for all grade levels. By teaching and reinforcing values that advance personal responsibility, rights of citizenship, and overall sociality, the unit firmly linked cultural identity to civics. The centerpiece of the Cultural Identity curriculum was the Values Program. The goal of the new curriculum: training youth to be peaceable and productive citizens for the benefit of national society. Below I discuss the launch of the Values Program in schools, but also how through popular media it reached a broader Salvadoran population. I examine the Values Program as a mechanism for generating shared values and beneficent social practices and as a productive site for further exploring the nexus of culture, state power, and international governance.

In 2000 when the Values Program was in its second year, I met with Reina Gladis de Galdamez, curriculum expert for MINED. She provided me with detailed information about the program and its content. The program had two components: Human and Ethical Values (Valores Humanos y Eticos) and Civic Values (Valores Civicos). Reina provided me with two sets of methodological guides (one for each component) used in the training of educators. Each set contained additional information pertaining to one of four levels: preschool (*parvularia*); first–third grades (*primer*); fourth–sixth grades (*segundo*); and seventh–ninth grades (*tercer*—also known as *bachillerato*). The guides listed particular social values and instructions for incorporating them "transversally," that is, teaching the values throughout all subject areas of the educational curriculum.

These are the fifteen human and ethical values contained in the program:

Work	Truthfulness	Generosity
Family Love	Strength	Charity
Cooperation	Order and Responsibility	Friendship
Honor	Respect	Loyalty
Obedience	Kindness	Life and Health

These are the eleven civic values:

Social Coexistence	The Common Good
Democratic Participation	Liberty and Democracy in our Schools
Respect of Others	Respect for Authority
Cultural Identity	Responsibility in the Community
Peace	Protection of Children
Solidarity	

In 1998 when Evelyn Jacir de Lovo, the minister of education, launched the Values Program throughout the school system, she named 1998 as "The Year of Values" (El Año de los Valores). This naming practice mimicked the UN method of linking the calendar to designated global themes. Colorful posters announced "I Have VALUE" (Yo Tengo VALOR), which, through the use of a clever acronym, introduced a few of the core values emphasized by the program.

Yo Tengo VALOR
V: Voluntad (will power)
A: Auto Estima (self-esteem)
L: Libertad (freedom)
O: Optimismo (optimism)
R: Responsibilidad (responsibility)

The posters were distributed foremost to all schools, but soon also appeared throughout El Salvador, cropping up in storefront windows and beyond.

For the 1999–2000 school year the thirty-six "human, ethical and civic" social values were incorporated into the academic calendar. In addition to celebrating an overarching "value of the year" and a "value of the month," there was a different value for each week of the school year. Educators were told to promote the weekly values in their teaching and make them resonate throughout the curriculum for any given week. Although teachers received some training in how this extraordinary feat might be accomplished, the transversal requirement rapidly became a major challenge, and educators complained of having insufficient training, guidelines, or concrete examples on how best to achieve the ambitious educational goals.

There was a requirement for students to perform civic acts (*actos civicos*) that reflected or embodied the value of the week. This activity was a formal performative aspect of students' training in the state-approved, socially accepted values. The civic acts took place during the school assembly and involved presentations by students who addressed their fellow students, teachers, and staff with a discussion of the designated value and its merit.[10] Through the promotion of values, including through such student performances, the Cultural Identity education attempted to socialize students in acceptable attitudes and behaviors and thereby, according to the government's policy goals, strengthen postwar national society. This point is made obvious in the pedagogical examples appearing in the methodological guides. Take, for example, the value "peace": the suggested phrase for reflection is "If peace is born in our heart, it could flower throughout the nation" (Si la paz nace en nuestro corazón podrá florecer en toda la nación).

In addition to the everyday classroom attention given to selected values, local popular media facilitated and reinforced the promotion of these values to the broader national society. The two largest daily newspapers, *La Prensa Gráfica* and *Diario de Hoy*, each launched campaigns to promote the Values Program, thus demonstrating that local media, though independent from government dictate, was an ally in this state-led nation-building project. From March to October 2000, *La Prensa Gráfica* held an essay contest on the topic "I Practice Values in My School and in My Community" (Practico Valores en Mi Escuela y en Mi Comunidad) and offered prizes to participating students. During that same time period, a two-page supplement "Let's Live Values" (Vamos a Vivir Valores) appeared every Thursday in that same newspaper. The colorful "collectible" supplement geared toward youth contained cartoons and puzzles, along with a short lesson on the particular MINED value of the week. Newspapers also communicated directly to educators by offering creative suggestions on how to illustrate or integrate a particular value into classroom activities.

Efforts promoting the Values Program specifically addressed parents as the audience. *Diario de Hoy* circulated the supplement "Children and Ourselves: Learning Human and Ethical Values" (Los Niños y Nosotros: Aprendiendo Valores Humanos y Eticos). The supplement emphasized the role of parents in socializing youth toward selected positive values and practices. The newspaper supplements also functioned as an informal mechanism for raising adult citizens' awareness of the same social values. The newspapers synchronized their educational materials with the MINED calendar of values. Thus in addition to aiding instruction in the classroom, the information provided by high circulation newspapers extended the education about beneficent values beyond the classroom with the aim of influencing a broader national public.

The above illustrates how two major newspapers supported state-led educational goals to promote and reinforce selected civic values. *La Prensa Gráfica* and *Diario de Hoy* have the largest readership of El Salvador's ten currently circulating newspapers. They are sold on nearly every street corner of San Salvador. They are considered mainstream newspapers. Neither is particularly critical of government policy, nor overly critical of El Salvador's gross poverty and social inequality. Still, having these two newspapers coordinate with MINED campaigns to promote cultural identity and selected values meant that a large portion of the Salvadoran population could literally be "on the same page" with one another to learn about and discuss the values that are important to Salvadoran youth and society in general.

The historical role of print media to foster national communities by enabling a population that will never be able to completely be acquainted face to face to share the same news, literature, or other information is central to Benedict Anderson's thesis of the emergence of nation-states and the formation of national identities (B. Anderson [1983] 2006). Today scholars continue to examine how popular media inform citizens of current affairs but also shape national narratives and subjectivities. Worth exploring is the role of the media in constituting publics, its relationships to states *and* markets, and the implication of media in hegemonic and counterhegemonic projects.[11]

Beyond newspapers, other media outlets in El Salvador also supported the state-led educational campaign. In the postwar years, television replaced radio as the primary public media source. In 2005 the UN reported more television receivers per capita in El Salvador than in any other Central American nation (Salzman and Salzman 2009).[12] It is logical that one particular television station, Canal 10, the state-run station for cultural and educational programming, would reinforce the Values Program. It did so through the weekly show *Letting You Know (Dando a Conocer)*. *Letting You Know*, filmed on a simple stage set with a colorful backdrop, introduced the television audience to a number of short segments that featured local attractions, national symbols, and selected values.

In addition, the radio program *Revista Cultural*, sponsored by the Association of Radio Broadcasters, aired daily at noon on nearly every radio station in El Salvador. While *Revista Cultural* was a major tool for increasing awareness of specific aspects of national culture and history, the broadcasts also directly referenced the selected weekly values promoted by the Values Program. In 1996 I interviewed Jorge Vargas Mendez, the principal force behind *Revista Cultural*. He conducted research and wrote the scripts for the daily radio program. He is also a dedicated poet, scholar, and founding member of El Salvador's Círculo Literario Xibalbá.[13] Vargas Mendez told me that he relished the opportunity to contribute to the strengthening of Salvadoran cultural and national identity through education and media. His approach differed from the Values Program in that his programming primarily celebrated the uniqueness of El Salvador. Another way that *Revista Cultural*'s programming was distinct was its emphasis on human rights issues and its form of challenging attitudes that reinforced social exclusion. *Revista Cultural* illustrated both universal and particular approaches to national culture and emphasized the vernacular and colloquial aspects of local cultural traditions such as *caliche*, the unique form of language spoken by Salvadorans that blends Spanish and indigenous words. After nearly fifteen years of daily broadcast *Revista Cultural* was taken off the air in January 2007 as the result of lack of continued funding.

Evaluating the Values Program

Through changes in curriculum, coordinated school practices, and the assistance of popular media, the Values Program was launched in El Salvador. To date it is obvious that it has not functioned as a panacea for uniting a polarized society or for transforming El Salvador's high incidence of crime, violence, and civil insecurity.[14] In El Salvador "peace-time crimes and violence" occur on what Nancy Scheper-Hughes and Philippe Bourgois (2004) refer to as a "continuum of violence between war and peace." On this continuum, the misrecognition of symbolic and structural violence, in acts both small and large, serves to naturalize the conditions of violence (Bourdieu 1977). Thus, although national cultural projects attempt to shape meanings, values, and practices, structural factors, including political and economic factors, can create unfavorable conditions that undermine the aims of state-led educational projects. The reality in El Salvador proves there can be a disjuncture between moral reasoning and moral behavior.[15]

One reason why the Values Program did not have a bigger impact was that it did not consider complex variables such as the particulars of history, the lack of equality, or the function of power in society. A general critique can be made of historical and contemporary nation-building efforts like the Culture of Peace Program or the Values Program that focus on creating shared values and meanings but that are not attentive to social structure and that do little to address pervasive inequalities.

It bears mentioning that scholars have examined the historically specific application and promotion of social norms and values to demonstrate the links between culture, society, and the power of government. From Friedrich Nietzsche (1967), who explored moral constructs of good and evil, to Michel Foucault (1977), who linked historical discourse about deviance to the social institutions that contend with unruly subjects, to Nikolas Rose's (2000) exposition about the uses of "freedom" for neoliberal economics and politics of empire, scholars have examined the social construction of norms and values and their use in social control and governance.[16] They reveal how the promotion of cultural values and norms produces subjectivities, and how their "enforcement" disciplines social subjects to adhere to normative behavior while serving to legitimate authority.

Whether values and norms function as benign "civilizing" processes or direct microtechnologies of self and social control, the reinforcement of selected values in El Salvador's postwar nation-building projects underscored the relationship between culture and power. Michel Foucault's concept of governmentality is useful for explaining this relationship between culture and power. It refers specifically to the power of the state to exert influence on the attitudes or comportment of citizens, as subjects, in less than direct ways, once citizens begin to self-monitor or police the behavior of others.[17] Thus while educational reform in El Salvador demonstrated the promotion of positive social values as a means to reconstruct postwar society, it also gave additional meaning to governmental goals to produce "perfect citizens." The postwar educational program that linked culture and values to the rights and duties of citizens also demonstrated the intimate link between culture, nation-building, and the strategies by which the state attempted to render members of society governable. The elite-imposed "values" can be critiqued on a number of fronts: (1) as a patriarchal, conservative initiative that marginalizes many women (single mothers in particular) within deeply impoverished populations; and (2) as a colonialist move linked to the neoliberal push toward self-empowerment where in addition to self-responsibility there can also be self-blame.

There were ongoing efforts in El Salvador to gauge the effectiveness of the Values Program and other simultaneously occurring state-led nation-building practices. Projects that assessed or evaluated certain state-led projects illustrated the role of social scientists, especially anthropologists. For example, in 1999 Salvadoran anthropologist Carlos Lara Martínez was hired to evaluate one aspect of the Values Program. Namely he was specifically asked to investigate how various social actors in a range of diverse educational settings were interpreting the value "cultural identity." Cultural identity stands out from the list of civic and ethical values because it is the one value that sought to make reference to El Salvador's unique cultural heritage as opposed to the other universally accepted and individually focused values. His research was sponsored by MINED, Fundación Empresarial Para el Desarrollo Educativo (a local nongovernmental organization devoted to educational development), and USAID. USAID funding is another example of international community interest and involvement in postwar social and cultural development efforts. Lara Martínez compared six representative schools: public/private, urban/rural, Catholic/Protestant. His research revealed mixed responses of students and teachers to the meaning of cultural identity. In his published study, Lara Martínez (1999) developed the following hypotheses about meanings held about national cultural identity in educational settings in El Salvador.

1. The discourse that the formal national educational system has developed for its unit on cultural identity is predominantly a folkloristic vision that favors traditional symbols (music, folklore, rural symbols, culture of the corn) over modern symbols. It is, however, one that recognizes the value of constructing a different conception of cultural identity that, without negating the value of the traditional or folkloric, seeks to locate

Salvadoran identity in the context of contemporary society, incorporating the dynamic of transnational society and culture.

2. Cultural identity values are different in accordance with the socioeconomic status of the educational actors.

3. There is an opposition between attitudes of youth and adults that produces significant ruptures in the meanings held about cultural identity.

4. Between national identity and local identities there exist contradictions that have to do with the configuration of economic, political, and cultural power in the nation, and these contradictions are expressed in the discourse about cultural identity.[18]

The study's principal discovery is that students have very different ideas than teachers or administrators about what constitutes cultural identity. Teachers and administrators in the study tended to define cultural identity as being not only about "where we come from," but "that which is truly our own" (*lo nuestro*). Educators did not connect national culture to the abstract universal values promoted throughout the Values Program. Instead they defined cultural identity in terms of symbols and concepts from El Salvador's past, whether a far-off pre-Hispanic or colonial past, or a more recent past. As such their responses were in alignment with the specific curricular content MINED established for the one value among the twenty-six program values that addressed El Salvador's local and particular cultural identity, whereas the majority of the values emphasized universal human values. "Cultural identity" reiterated the importance of history, archaeological sites, customs, traditions, and language. Yet some teachers equated cultural identity in El Salvador with historical and contemporary processes of acculturation, noting transformations from original indigenous culture to Spanish culture, and commenting strongly that today's society is unduly influenced by North American culture. These teachers' responses defined cultural identity primarily as an absence of "our own culture."

The responses of students, however, were more general and less critical. They tended to see cultural identity as "representing persons from here—where we are born and where we pass the majority of our time; our culture; customs and traditions; and language" (Lara Martinez 1999). A notable difference in overall student response, however, was from students in rural schools. Here both urban life and transnational influences were seen as something distant from conceptions of "authentic" national culture or identity.

As Lara Martínez's study indicates, the Values Program set out to promote a particular set of universally accepted beneficent social values, but included one unit on cultural identity that emphasized the particularities of Salvadoran culture. However, the selected values were being received by students and adults (teachers, parents, and general population alike) from diverse socioeconomic and subcultural worlds who filtered the educational social and cultural development project through their distinct social positioning and experiences of what it means to be from El Salvador. While the history of modern nation-building can be understood in terms of the successful or hegemonic projects to shape collective understandings about national culture and society, the reality is that diverse interests arise to agree with or challenge dominant, state-led efforts. My project of following state-led practices of nation-building in El Salvador required me to be attentive to differences, disagreements, and the local criticism that emerged about the Values Program.

Local Critique of the Values Program

On April 5, 2000, *La Prensa Gráfica* published an editorial opinion piece by Evelyn Jacir de Lovo, then minister of education. It was titled "Why is perseverance the value for 2000?" (¿Por qué la perseverancia es el valor para el 2000?). Jacir de Lovo was responding to brewing criticism against the Values Program among cultural elites and certain government officials. These critics held that the Values Program, then in its second year, overly emphasized universal values, including democratic culture, at the expense of attending to what is special about El Salvador. They lamented that the lack of attention to El Salvador's uniqueness meant a continuation of historical practices whereby government and elites imitated external models and allowed external interests to influence national dynamics. In the editorial Jacir de Lovo attempted to persuade her critics that the Values Program would, in fact, generate feelings of being "authentically

Salvadoran." It would do so by forming character, and this formation of character would make the citizenry feel "authentically Salvadoran." Further, this authenticity would connect to a sense of belonging to national society. This tenuous logic, however, did not convince the critics, and many continued to lobby for government education policies to focus more attention on local culture, history, and the unique identity of the nation.

As the reference above suggests, one method by which I followed the growing local critique of the Values Program and other state-led nation-building efforts was through the daily newspapers, especially by monitoring the opinion-editorial pages and the letters to the editor. The daily newspaper served as a forum where the relatively small cadre of local cultural elites shared their perspectives on contemporary society, including their views about the Values Program. One recurring theme I noted in these newspaper forums was the pairing of the educational program's promotion of "new" values against "anti-values" (*anti-valores*), which were perceived as rampant in postwar society. Other letter writers did not pit anti-values against new values. Instead they identified the enduring structural factors that maintained poverty and marginalization and prevented El Salvador from achieving the social standards promoted by the Values Program. Some letter writers communicated that the program placed too much attention on the role of the individual and the individual's behavior and attitude. Others noted that the program did not acknowledge El Salvador's history of repressive government, did not mention the recent civil war, made no reference to the harsh economic realities, and did not address gross social inequality as possible factors that impeded social cohesion and unity. Similar to my general discussion above about the program's shortcomings, critics in El Salvador claimed that MINED lacked attention to the key factors that warped any social contract.

In July 2000 I attended a MINED public forum about the Values Program. The approximately 150 people present exceeded the available seating, forcing many of us to stand. The energy in the meeting room was electric. It was not the first time I had experienced this dynamic at government-sponsored meetings. Then-president Francisco Flores's administration was almost frantic to convey to the public its commitment to a policy of inclusive and open government. In addition, I had the sense that a huge clock was running down for the Flores administration to prove that it could be effective in implementing new programs and charting a course for improving El Salvador's precarious economic and social conditions. Flores's ARENA party was losing the confidence of Salvadoran voters. The country had just completed nonpresidential elections, and the FMLN (no longer the guerrilla opposition force but now a bona fide political party) won enough votes to earn nearly 50 percent overall representation at municipal, departmental, and national levels of government. MINED officials, like others in government, felt intense pressure to show results and to change negative public attitudes about government and its performance.

The audience at the meeting I attended was comprised primarily of teachers who had responded to the MINED announcement in the daily newspapers urging them to attend. After a few congratulatory remarks by MINED officials on teachers' efforts to promote values, attention turned to the practical difficulties of realizing the program's pedagogical objectives. A microphone-wielding MINED staff member worked his way through the crowded forum to provide audience members with a chance to share their viewpoints. A number of teachers in the audience complained that the requirement to make the value of the month and the value of the year resonate through the entire curriculum was the biggest challenge. How to make it happen was proving formidable. They asked if specific exercises could be drawn up and provided for them, because the effort of imagining creative tie-ins that allowed values to be promoted alongside the instruction of other academic subjects was proving to be overwhelming. The MINED staff seemed sympathetic and solicited additional testimonials from members of the audience, who expressed various degrees of success and frustration. Soon there was consensus that the concept of the Values Program was far ahead of its practical application. Rather than a disheartening revelation, it was viewed as a developmental issue for a worthwhile program still in its infancy.

As teachers and administrators at the forum collectively explored the Values Program, one particular reaction stood out. Near the end of time scheduled for the public forum, off in one corner of the meeting room, a concerned teacher's hand shot up in the audience. Once the microphone arrived, the teacher spoke:

> While no one can object to the promotion of cultural values, these are universal values, not Salvadoran values. So what about our culture, our unique national culture? This is where we should look to find the solution to our society's problems not just in universal values. We Salvadorans are a unique people, and it is in our unique heritage, our indigenous ancestry, that we must look to find the pure spirit of our national identity.

Some in the audience nodded their heads in agreement, and some murmured approval. Others, though, did not attempt to hide their disdain for such a "preposterous" notion as looking to indigenous heritage for national inspiration.

The teacher's comments did resonate with a frequent criticism I encountered while researching the Values Program. The criticism did not come from the person on the street or from the media, but primarily from within MINED. A subtle rejection of the Values Program came from administrators working in Consejo Nacional Para la Cultura y el Arte (CONCULTURA), which was then a subdivision of MINED but is today independent in the form of the newly created Secretariat of Culture. CONCULTURA advocated a different perspective on culture in postwar nation-building projects. Instead of culture based on the promotion of universal civic and social values of citizenship for a democratic society, CONCULTURA advocated projects based on an essential, primordial culture over time that linked the national population with state and territory. As mentioned earlier in this chapter, such a strategy instrumentalizes the concept of culture. It was in favor of recognizing a deeply rooted past and El Salvador's unique present-day cultural identity, one traced back to pre-Hispanic times and to Nahuat, Lenca, Cacaopera, and Maya indigenous heritage. This, they argued, ought to be the basis of efforts to strengthen social unity and represent national belonging. Thus in addition to the Values Program another simultaneously occurring state-led approach to postwar nation-building was focused instead on El Salvador's unique ethnic and racial cultural heritage.

Conclusion

The wariness that some Salvadorans expressed about the universal aspects of the Values Program demonstrates how globalized strategies of international intervention confront local response and dynamics. On one level, the public debates and criticism that surround the Values Program are located on a long historical continuum of nation-building efforts in El Salvador. How to define the nation was as contentious an endeavor now as it had been throughout the history of the nation-state. On another level, the political and economic spheres of El Salvador had also long been subjected to significant external political, economic, and cultural influence. Even when not explicitly stated as such, local concerns about El Salvador's sovereignty and autonomy were thus inevitable.

I have argued that UNESCO's influence on El Salvador showed the role of the international community to shape the postwar nation, especially through goals to influence students' subjectivities, behaviors, and identities through schooling. Other scholars have critiqued the Culture of Peace Program's focus on individual thought and behavior as being a form of global regulation in the formation of "global" citizens (Ilcan and Phillips 2006). Certainly the proposed program and MINED's derivative Values Program lacked attention to El Salvador's history, social structure, and inequality. Further, by involving a strategy to form citizens who are first and foremost individuals, who are prepared to participate as laborers in the global economy and as citizens in free-market democracies, the approach to fostering democratic culture mirrors ideals of neoliberalism.

In addition to regulating students and citizens, we can view the program as also reinforcing certain positive expectations for the government of El Salvador. The internationally sanctioned teaching of culture, civics, and participation in a global democratic society concomitantly disciplined the state about adherence to democratic norms. This showed up, for example, in the reinforcement of the values of "democratic participation," "protection of children," and "respect for others." Considering the repressive history of El Salvador, including decades of military dictatorship, these values remind citizens of the responsibility of government. Further, it must be noted, in order to be ensured of further international aid, upon which El

Salvador depends, the state must demonstrate a degree of conformity to the ideals of democratic society. On a less positive note, El Salvador's adherence to current global policies, including economic neoliberalism that relies on scaled-back state services and the privatization of national resources, affects the extent to which UNESCO and other international entities engage El Salvador.

The tensions that arose in El Salvador over how to adequately represent national culture through the educational system illuminated the diverse actors, interests, and competing ideas involved in the dynamic and ongoing process of nation-building. This helps to explain why in El Salvador a number of simultaneously occurring state-led projects represented the meaning of national belonging. This chapter emphasized an approach based primarily on the promotion of universally accepted, individually based cultural values. The next chapter demonstrates how nation-building practices that focused attention on national history and specificity were designed to emphasize El Salvador's uniqueness. Most of the projects depended on ancient indigenous culture and heritage to symbolize national belonging. Indigeneity, a strategy for instrumentalizing concepts of unique culture and nation, and its relation to post–civil war ideas of the nation are explored next.

2

Drawing on the Past

History, Archaeology, Inclusions, and Exclusions

Pastness is a central element in the socialization of individuals, in the maintenance of group solidarity, in the establishment of or challenge to social legitimation. Pastness therefore is preeminently a moral phenomenon, therefore a political phenomenon, always a contemporary phenomenon.
—*Immanuel Wallerstein, 1991: 78.*

IN POSTWAR EL SALVADOR, there were simultaneously occurring state-led projects to represent the nation and rebuild national society. Some nation-building strategies looked to El Salvador's deep past for symbols of the unique nation. The approach is familiar to some Latin American nations, such as Mexico, and actually revived an early twentieth-century strategy promoted by the state in El Salvador.

For all modern societies, the past, as Immanuel Wallerstein attests, is a rich reservoir explored by those charged with the design and promotion of nation-building. Yet what is recalled is a selective and partial past, and necessarily so. Codified versions of the past are frequently touted as national histories, and acceptance of official representations of the past is a cornerstone of modern nation-building. Challengers campaign for alternative depictions of notable days and events gone by, or decry exclusions in the official versions of

44

yesteryear. As such, pastness, so essential to communicating shared meanings about the nation and national belonging, is steeped in issues of power and authority and marked by inclusion and exclusion.

For state-led nation-building in El Salvador, addressing the past, albeit a selective one, was a priority. While official silence about the atrocities of the civil war continued, presumably to quell tensions in a society split apart by its violence, uniting the national population around other shared pasts became essential. Also, emphasizing a distinctly Salvadoran past was thought by some to combat outside influences. Local critics claimed national society was increasingly pulled into a global cultural sphere and that globalization eroded El Salvador's distinctiveness. As the past was harvested for evidence, markers, and reminders of the unique nation, there was new institutional support for the practices that produced historical knowledge and shared meanings. In addition to launching the nation's first academic programs in history and anthropology, the postwar government demonstrated strong support for archaeology and the window it opened onto the deep past.

This chapter examines state-led practices drawing new attention to the nation's social and cultural past. Some projects included international actors and audiences. Archaeological investigations and plans for managing archaeological sites involved international experts, and new sites showcased the nation's past to attract foreign tourists. International partners aiding the preservation of the archaeological site Joya de Cerén suggested, for example, that the site's care would require a national society that understands the intrinsic value of the site and the past it represents. This suggestion returns us to the postwar emphasis on the promotion and construction of values explored in chapter 1.

Postwar projects represented the nation exclusively through the history of indigenous populations, Spaniards, and mestizos (those of mixed indigenous and Spanish heritage). This exemplified the Latin American ideology of mestizaje, where the fusion of Spaniards and indigenous people is celebrated as creating a unique national race, and the ancient indigenous past is exalted.[1] Although mestizaje underpinned recent promotions of the unique nation, the postwar state-led efforts actually mirrored decades-earlier nation-building practices. Although the postwar government promoted the deep past by highlighting the pre-Columbian heritage of El Salvador, contemporary indigenous ethnic minorities continued to be excluded and marginalized. State-led strategies to emphasize El Salvador's cultural history also ignored the presence of other ethnic and racial groups. Excluded in representations of the nation were references to historical migrations to El Salvador from Africa, the Middle East, the Far East, Western Europe, and elsewhere. My study of how the past was selectively used as a resource for nation-building, therefore, required attention to inclusions as well as exclusions, and to competing interests that complicated any assumption that promoting a shared past would unite a divided national society.

History and Anthropology Matter

On June 18, 2000, at the reception hall of the National Museum of Anthropology (Museo Nacional de Antropología (MUNA), a museum so new that the exhibition halls were not yet fully open to the public, a well-dressed crowd assembled in the sunset hours. From all accounts this was a unique and momentous gathering of local elites. Politicians, poets, patrons of the arts, and members of the media mingled with local and international scholars, representatives of governmental and nongovernmental organizations, and state officials. Sparking the gala was the inauguration of the Fifth Congress of Central American History, held for the first time in El Salvador.[2] Coordinated by the University of El Salvador's Institute of Historical, Anthropological, and Archaeological Studies, the Congress (June 18–21, 2000) brought together participants from seventeen countries and more than fifty universities.

The highbrow gathering was a celebration of El Salvador's intellectual attention to social and cultural priorities. Delivering the inaugural keynote address was David Browning, a geographer from Oxford University. Browning's *El Salvador: Landscape and Society* (1971) remains a standard text in classrooms of higher education in El Salvador. Before a rapt audience, Browning commented on how much El Salvador had changed since the days of his early research. After praising the nation's emergence from civil war, he enumerated what he found to be the most pressing challenges for the nation:

increasing urbanization, escalating population growth, and the perilous erosion of natural resources. His presentation was lauded. However, the highlight of the evening was the presentation of Dr. Evelyn Rodriquez, rector of the University of El Salvador, who received a standing ovation when she announced that the national university was about to launch El Salvador's first academic degree program for the study of history.

Prior to 2000, El Salvador offered no formal academic opportunities to study history. That fact makes El Salvador unusual among modern nation-states. Nation-building has often relied on local scholars to produce powerful narratives of the nation's past, and because such representations of the past often serve official interests, historians and historiography have held important legitimating functions in many modern nations. The timing of El Salvador's new attention to history, in the peak of postwar nation-building, is, however, noteworthy.

It is important to note that although the Universidad de El Salvador is a public university and funded by the government, the campus in San Salvador was a major site of confrontation and protest against the state violence that triggered the civil war as its knowledge producers struggled against state hegemony. For example, the revolutionary poet Roque Dalton challenged the lies and omissions of the received version of Salvadoran history. Two of Dalton's most cited works: *Historias prohibidas del pulgarcito*[3] (1974), and *El Salvador: Mongrafia* (1989) continue to influence ideas about the nation today. Historian Jorge Arias Gómez also critiqued national inequality and exclusion through scholarship that includes: "Anastasio Aquino: Su recuerdo, valoración y presencia" (1964); *Farabundo Martí: Esbozo biográfico* ([1972] 2004); and *En memoria de Roque Dalton* (1999). These and other individuals associated with the Universidad de El Salvador prior to and into the civil war conflict demonstrate the university as an important site of oppositional knowledge production during very turbulent times. Two recent books, *Remembering a Massacre in El Salvador* (2007) by Héctor Lindo-Fuentes, Erik Ching, and Rafael Lara-Martínez, and *To Rise in Darkness: Revolution, Repression, and Memory in El Salvador 1920–1932* (2008) by Jeffrey L. Gould and Aldo A. Lauria-Santiago provide valuable background information on some past struggles to tell the story of the nation. During the period of my fieldwork I noted that as the relationship between the state and the university slowly improved, the government gradually released desperately needed funding for repairs to the infrastructure that had suffered before the war had begun. I argue that the investment in new academic programs is linked to renewed state support for the university as well as to related postwar nation-building policies.

Despite the past absence of formal academic programs for the study of history, the University of El Salvador maintained as a research unit the Institute for Historical, Anthropological, and Archaeological Studies. In 1995 the institute published *Bibliografía Historiografica de El Salvador,* a slight volume that lists all known texts and publications on the topic of El Salvador's past, including key figures, events, and their representation. My research has benefited from visits to the Institute and from ongoing conversations over the years with its directors, former directors, and affiliated scholars, including Jorge Arias Gómez, Gregorio Bello Suazo, and Carlos Lara Martínez. Also deserving acknowledgment is the important work of Salvadoran Héctor Lindo-Fuentes, whose contributions are made from the diaspora (Gudmundson and Lindo-Fuentes 1995; Lindo-Fuentes 1990, 2003); and the research of respected scholars in El Salvador who work outside of the academy (Escalante Arce 1992; Walter 1998; Williams and Walter 1997).

In the early days of my research I spent three months in El Salvador's National Library surveying the collection for extant references to national history by Salvadoran scholars. Scanning for works from the mid-nineteenth century to the present, I identified forty-five history-related sources. The scholarship falls into one of four general categories: (1) political economy of the region; (2) focus on key individuals involved in regional and national independence movements; (3) studies of national culture, such as folklore, music, and dance; and (4) ethnographic surveys of local indigenous communities. The postwar period brought awareness of the gaps in scholarship, and certain entities of the national government, universities, and local and international scholars responded by emphasizing the importance of history for the nation. This included restoration of historical archives at the National Palace. Historian Aldo Lauria-Santiago (1995) produced a valuable summary and review of the archives and related resources.

The civil war ended in 1992 and by 1994 a new two-volume national history textbook, *Historia de El Salvador* (Government of El Salvador 1994), had been published. A multidisciplinary team of historians, archaeologists, and specialists in international relations and economy collaborated on its production. Some of these scholars were from El Salvador but did not reside in El Salvador at the time, having been dispersed around the world as a result of the civil war. The authors, while recognizing that it filled a public need for scholarship, had no pretensions that the new textbook was definitive. In fact, the *Historia de El Salvador* was praised for its critical approach to key topics and for a pedagogical openness that invited new interpretations and fresh understandings of past events. Considering that the scholars who co-authored the new text were on the political Left, undoubtedly negotiations with Ministry of Education (MINED) or other government officials ensued to constrain what would otherwise be a strong critique of a history of state repression, oligarchy, and social inequality. That said, in the introduction to the first volume, Cecilia Gallardo de Cano, then minister of education, expressed the expectation that learning about El Salvador's history will consolidate shared meanings about national belonging:

> We need to reconstruct the past. That from millennia past, that of the conquest, that of the colony, that of our modern nation and even more recent. We have to enrich the collective memory. A new conscience about the NATURE of our nationality requires a historical perspective. And it is this effort, modest but honest, converted into text about the HISTORY OF EL SALVADOR that the Ministry of Education contributes to the consolidation of this new conscience.[4] (Emphasis in original, my translation.)

Historia de El Salvador was widely distributed throughout the nation and continues to serve as the primary reference for national history in all schools in El Salvador. The cover illustration for volume 1 features an excavated structure from the archaeological site Joya de Cerén. Chapter 1 commences with a discussion of the earliest known inhabitants in the region. The slender volume 1 swiftly leads the reader from the pre-Columbian past, through colonialism, to nineteenth-century independence. For postwar El Salvador, it became clear that national history would begin with the ancient past.

Anthropology Matters

Anthropology, too, formally arrived in postwar El Salvador. In 2004 the University of El Salvador initiated the nation's first program for the study of sociocultural anthropology, while the private Universidad Tecnológica introduced separate programs in anthropology and archaeology. Anthropology actively engages with history and as such is fundamental to nation-building practices. Biological or physical anthropology attempts to reconstruct the history of human evolution. Through ethnohistory anthropologists study how people represent their origins or unique past. Historical anthropology and historical archaeology study aspects of past social worlds that are not revealed or are often overlooked by other research fields. Standard archaeology often researches "prehistory," unearthing material to construct narratives about societies not represented in the work of modern historians. As such, the social science of anthropology can be instrumental in providing the "evidence" about the past upon which modern nation-states often stake claims.

To look reflexively at anthropology, however, means to consider the social and political context of the production of anthropological knowledge. It requires anthropologists to identify the interests served by any particular narratives of the past (or present) based on the findings of anthropological research. Archaeologists, in particular, are increasingly aware of how the products of their research serve political projects of nation-building (Joyce 2003; Kane 2003; Trigger 1996). Previously, some archaeologists distanced themselves from contemporary concerns by defining their projects in terms of temporally distant societies. Today it is clear that archaeological research is linked to contemporary sociopolitical concerns and interests and a range of different players, no matter how archaeologists themselves frame their work. This has required a new attentiveness, if not accountability, by archaeologists to the contemporary communities attached to archaeological sites. Julia Herndon and Rosemary Joyce (2004) produced a textbook on Mesoamerican archaeology that actively advocates placing contemporary communities within the archaeological research design in order to address the contemporary context, impact, importance, and audience of archaeological research.

Scholarship today reflects upon the historical development of the practice of archaeology and its service to the goals of nationalism (Joyce 2003; Kane 2003; Kohl and Fawcett 1996; Trigger 1996). With the surging academic interest in nation-states, national identities, and nationalism, the links between the production of knowledge about the nation and its past draw archaeologists, their research sites, and the knowledge they produce into the sphere of nation-building processes. In El Salvador, the practice and products of archaeology had a prominent new role in the service of postwar nation-building.

Along with El Salvador's enhanced interest in national history and historiography, archaeology was recognized for its ability to influence shared meanings about the nation and national belonging. The new Secretariat of Culture (formerly CONCULTURA) is charged with protecting and promoting a vast inventory of national patrimony, including archaeological sites. Currently there are 340 registered archaeological sites in El Salvador and probably 800 or more that have been identified but not yet registered. At the time of this research the government managed seven archaeological sites: Joya de Cerén, San Andrés, Tazumal, Casa Blanca, Cara Sucia, Cihuatán, and La Gruta del Espíritu Santo. Management by the government means that the state owns the land, hires the staff to care for the sites, and receives all monies generated by promotion, tourism, or research at the sites. In return, the state through the Secretariat of Culture is responsible for maintaining, preserving, and restoring the registered archaeological sites.

In the past only foreign archaeologists investigated El Salvador's principal sites (Boggs 1943a, 1943b, 1944; Bruhns 1976, 1980; Coe 1955; Fowler 1984; McKee 1999; Sheets 1989, 1992; among others).[5] El Salvador did not have the resources to undertake extensive archaeological investigations, and there were no local opportunities to train Salvadorans in archaeology. These factors persuaded the government to allow foreign archaeologists to excavate. Since 1991, however, the caveat for foreign archaeologists wishing to conduct fieldwork on Salvadoran soil is that they must hire and train locals in archaeology.

Now foreign archaeologists proposing projects for El Salvador confront a strong nationalism. Still, the role of foreign archaeologists was critical to the development of archaeology in postwar El Salvador. Salvadoran archaeologist Roberto Gallardo received his on-the-job training from University of Kyoto archaeologists who conducted Project Chalchuapa in western El Salvador from 1997 to 2000. The project incorporated archaeology, ethnohistory, and ethnographic research at the pre-Maya site of Casa Blanca (300 BCE–200 CE) and nearby surroundings. This project trained many of El Salvador's first generation of archaeologists such as Gallardo, some of whom also studied in Japan to complete their training. Karen O. Bruhns, professor of archaeology at San Francisco State University in California, resumed research at Cihuatán in 1993, a project that had been interrupted by the civil war. Similarly, Payson Sheets of the University of Colorado at Boulder resumed research at Joya de Cerén, one of Central America's most remarkable archaeological sites, a project that was also disrupted by war. Since 1996 William Fowler of Vanderbilt University has conducted excavations of the historical site of Ciudad Vieja, the first permanently occupied colonial site named San Salvador; his research evidences the presence of multiethnic, multinational indigenous populations. Today these archaeologists advance their scholarship while training and employing Salvadorans as members of their research teams.[6]

The archaeological site of Joya de Cerén tests concerns that I heard expressed by individuals working in CONCULTURA about who will value El Salvador's past more, "the world" or Salvadorans. The site is a complex of at least seventeen structures buried under five meters of volcanic ash. The interred hamlet is approximately 1,400 years old. The blanket of ash preserved the quality of the site's material culture, and it provides extraordinary details of the daily life of a nonelite population. Compared to the monumental archaeological sites through which we typically experience ancient Mesoamerica, Joya de Cerén provides an unrivalled glimpse into the past. To date, a handful of structures have been unearthed. Nicknamed the "Pompeii of the Americas," Cerén continues to receive international attention. In 1993 it was designated a UNESCO World Heritage Site. Since then, El Salvador's postwar government has invested educational, media, and tourism development resources to convert the site into a valuable symbol of the nation. From the early days of the postwar period, Joya de Cerén was in the imagination of those charged with rebuilding the nation. From 1992 forward, CONCULTURA and MINED promoted Joya de Cerén as national patrimony, while the state's tourism development infrastructure converted the site into the crown jewel of national tourism development. The links between archaeology, tourism, and national identity were not underestimated by the Salvadoran state. For nation-states that look to tourism revenues as a source of economic development, the value of archaeology as a resource for national heritage and as an attraction for international visitors (in particular diasporic nationals returning as "tourists") further justified state efforts to prioritize it.

Until the postwar period the government of El Salvador had invested little in the practice of national historiography or the products of archaeology. This contrasts with the strategies of other Latin American nation-states that established ties to the past, in particular to the deep past, in order to legitimate claims to territory, resources, and even to cultural regimes. While reaching for modernity, it was not unusual for nineteenth- and twentieth-century nation-builders to assert primordial ties to national territory (B. Anderson [1983] 2006; Brading 1993; Earle 2007; Gamio [1916] 1982; Thurner 1997). It is important to note that most nation-states wielding claims based on ties to ancient civilizations, however, have been ambivalent, at best, about the status of their contemporary indigenous populations. Analisa Taylor (2009), who researches this dynamic in the history of Mexico's cultural imagination, refers to ways that indigenous people are treated as "fickle" and "contradictory." This is an apt description of state practices taking place in postwar El Salvador.

Today the government of El Salvador emphasizes indigeneity, symbolized by the nation's pre-Columbian past. However, the efforts rest a bit uncomfortably alongside elite attitudes that, while promoting mestizaje, looked first to Western Europe and then to the United States for ideals of modernity, progress, and race-based values of social hierarchy. These elite attitudes distanced Salvadorans from indigenous cultural heritage and did little to promote an interest in the nation's unique past. Many Salvadorans I interviewed decried this tendency of elites and others to value outside influences over domestic expressions, a mind-set that also showed up, for example, in Lara Martínez's research on divergent ideas about cultural identity discussed in the previous chapter.

Nonetheless, in postwar El Salvador, state practices that promoted the archaeological site of Joya de Cerén illustrated how the past was mobilized as a resource that served a myriad of functions. The site represented ideas about the uniqueness of shared national history, culture, and identity that could possibly forge solidarity. It also established El Salvador's foothold in regional Maya tourism projects such as Mundo Maya (Maya World) and Ruta Maya (Maya Route). "Maya" became a metonym for a diversity of indigenous cultures in a region whose complex deep history remains to be studied and understood and that increasingly provides evidence that migration and trade transformed it into a pre-Columbian cultural frontier. For postwar El Salvador, however, the grandeur of ancient Maya civilization became firmly attached to Joya de Ceren's heritage, while as a new tourist site it served as an economic resource (DeLugan 1994). As a UNESCO World Heritage Site, Joya de Cerén drew global attention. Images of Joya de Cerén were ubiquitous in El Salvador, appearing on national postage stamps and adorning the nation's currency prior to 2000, and they continue to be emblazoned on products for tourist consumption such as T-shirts, towels, crafts, and postcards.

Measuring the Value of Archaeology

There is no guarantee that promoting a shared archaeological past will produce present-day national solidarity. The government of El Salvador attempted to gauge the power of Joya de Cerén to serve as a symbol of the nation. As they assessed the cultural value of Joya de Cerén, they involved international actors whose participation in the care, maintenance, and planning of archaeological sites offers another angle on the global context of twenty-first-century nation-building.

Joya de Cerén, located in the Zapotitán Valley of western El Salvador, was discovered in the summer of 1978 when a local resident's bulldozer uncovered two structures buried beneath several meters of volcanic ash. The civil war interrupted early archaeological investigations led by the University of Colorado at Boulder. From 1989 to 1994 excavations resumed and revealed domestic structures that dated back at least 1,400 years. As mentioned above, in 1993 Joya de Cerén became a UNESCO World Heritage Site. It is, however, a fragile site. Renewed exposure to the elements is eroding the adobe and wattle-and-daub architecture of the site. Experiments with conservation treatments accompanied rigorous monitoring of the physical conditions of the excavated structures. Experts in the Conservation Analytical Laboratory at the Smithsonian Institution assisted with Joya de Cerén's conservation.

The Getty Conservation Institute (GCI), another international partner, worked with CONCULTURA to plan the future management of Joya de Cerén. The GCI's role in El Salvador connected with the regional interstate Maya Initiative (Iniciativa Maya). The broader project aimed to foster collaboration among the various countries of the Maya region (Mexico, Guatemala, Honduras, El Salvador, and Belize) to enhance cultural resource conservation training and practices. Extending beyond the physical care and conservation of fragile archaeological structures was the important issue of "value recognition." Value recognition referred to the extent to which locals cherished their archaeological cultural resources. The GCI contended that value recognition was essential to sustain support and commitment for conservation. International interest, such as the designation of UNESCO World Heritage Site, showed value recognition, but this recognition did not necessarily equate with local attitudes or values. The Maya Initiative contended that weak values could be strengthened and nonexistent values created. As with the Culture of Peace Program and Values Program outlined in chapter 1, there was an emphasis on the role of culture and cultural processes: If important social and cultural values were deemed absent, state efforts were directed toward nurturing and cultivating the values through curricula and media campaigns.

Component 1 of the Maya Initiative specifically focused on support for Joya de Cerén.[7] Between 1992 and 2002 CONCULTURA and GCI embarked on a participatory process to develop a site management plan for Joya de Cerén. A major first step was to determine Joya de Cerén's value recognition. Diagnosing the public's valuation of the site would also provide insight about other state projects focused on promoting the nation's unique past. The staff of CONCULTURA and GCI developed a survey that inquired about Joya de

Cerén, identification with Maya heritage, school attitudes regarding national history, identity, and even awareness of the existence and role of CONCULTURA and MINED. The survey was conducted with educators at thirteen public schools. Similar to anthropologist Carlos Lara Martínez's research on the meaning of "cultural identity" (discussed in chapter 1), the survey focused on a variety of schools, public, private, and religious, and schools located in metropolitan San Salvador and in the San Juan Opico area surrounding Joya de Cerén.

The archaeology staff at MUNA graciously gave me access to the raw data from the Maya Initiative survey. Below I summarize some of the survey results. In order to illustrate the range of responses elicited, including those demonstrating an attachment to indigenous cultural heritage and those expressing the opposite, I provide representative responses to particular questions. For example, to the question "How do Salvadorans see Maya Culture?" one educator from Canton Joya de Cerén (a rural unincorporated area very near the archaeological site) replied: "The students identify with the pre-Hispanic cultures and are not ashamed to say that they are their ancestors. . . . Salvadorans negate our identity, even though our customs are indigenous, and besides that the identity has been robbed."[8]

Another educator from nearby Canton San Andres responded: "Really nobody identifies as a descendent of the Maya. There is no identification with something like Mundo Maya. Instead we wish to be descended from the Spanish."

When educators from a school in metropolitan San Salvador were asked, "How do Salvadorans see Maya culture?" their responses ranged from "They view it as their own" to "They associate it with Mexico, Guatemala, and Honduras." These diverse responses illustrated the challenges for state nation-building efforts to generate shared meanings, affective ties, and national affinity based on the promotion of a common ancient indigenous heritage.

The majority of Salvadorans can be considered mestizos, meaning they are the cultural and biological product of the merging of indigenous societies and Spanish colonizers. The physiognomy of most Salvadorans reveals their Native American inheritance. Dominant society, however, disparages that racialized identity. Some educators and scholars in El Salvador discussed the unwillingness that some Salvadorans have toward embracing indigenous cultural heritage as a problem of *transculturación*, or transculturalization.[9] They used the concept to refer to the historical processes whereby Salvadorans adopted the culture of others (by force, by choice, or by hegemony). Transculturalization was blamed for robbing Salvadorans of their unique identity. Many educators participating in the Maya Initiative Survey stated that students today were indifferent to their own culture and history because of the influence of "North American culture." Others attributed Salvadorans' distance from their indigenous roots to a basic lack of knowledge of Maya culture and the tendency of Salvadorans to discriminate against indigenous populations.[10] Reasons for the lack of knowledge showed up in the answer that some gave to the question: "What are students being taught about history?" A typical response to that question was expressed by an educator from the rural Canton San Andres: "For teaching about the history of our country, there is neither adequate nor sufficient material from the Ministry of Education."

The Maya Initiative Survey revealed that educators considered questions of cultural identity crucial to Salvadorans. When asked the value of the pre-Hispanic past to education in El Salvador, one educator viewed it as necessary for strengthening cultural identity. Another educator commented that because it was of little importance to the government, it was of little importance to national education.

In spite of conflicting ideas, the overall survey responses demonstrated that the educational process on the whole in postwar El Salvador was assigning more value to pre-Columbian history. More responses indicated that the archaeological site of Joya de Cerén was valued and that the site generated interest and enthusiasm. Yet this simple diagnostic survey also demonstrated many of the concerns and debates held by state officials and cultural elites about postwar society. Were Salvadorans disconnected from their cultural roots? Had outside influences weakened national culture and identity? Was the denial of indigenous cultural heritage to blame for the loss of national identity? Would a new emphasis on indigenous heritage strengthen a sense of national belonging? Alongside the questions and concerns of state actors involved with postwar nation-building in El Salvador is the scholarly critique about the contemporary con-struction of collective identity; the dynamics of race, ethnicity, and nation; and how archaeological constructions of past worlds take on new meaning for contemporary states as well as segments of society who may contest hegemonic national identity projects. My goal is not to over-simplify the ongoing processes observed in El Salvador, but to highlight the complexities and even contradictions of the use of indigenous heritage as a basis for postwar national identity.

Hidden Histories: Beyond Indians and Mestizos

History textbooks and archaeological sites represented El Salvador's past and incited discussions about the meaning of national belonging. Indigenous cultural heritage was the primary focus for many postwar nation-building campaigns. Ambiguity, however, surrounded this strategy: some related to El Salvador's native roots and embraced indigeneity, while others who could claim the past demonstrated disdain for celebrating indigeneity as national heritage. While some identified with ancient indigenous heritage, they might still reject the notion that indigenous populations exist in present-day El Salvador and/or uphold the marginal social status of contemporary indigenous people. Still other Salvadorans will not see themselves at all in this particular representation of national history, culture, and identity.

These differing stances reveal the tension of race, ethnicity, and nation in El Salvador. To accurately present the diversity of postwar El Salvador requires a fuller view of history and culture than that currently offered. It means contending with what Salvadoran scholar Francisco Andres Escobar refers to as the nation's "turbios hilos de sangre" (disturbing or muddy bloodlines) (Escobar 1994). Escobar is drawing attention to society's refusal to acknowledge the African roots that accompanied slavery and colonization, the fact and fiction of whether and when black bodies were barred from the modern na-tion,[11] and the historical and ongoing subordination of indigenous populations. In the postwar years, there remained little reflection on these topics or other aspects of racial and ethnic diversity in Salva-doran society. The prevailing tendency was to keep hidden histories hidden.

Some ethnic histories may be hidden, but just barely beneath the surface. In 2004 Antonio Saca and Sharfik Handal faced off as opponents for the presidency of El Salvador. Both were Palestinian-Salvadorans. Handal was the son of Palestinian immigrants and Saca was the grandson of Palestinian immigrants. These facts were neither hidden nor celebrated. However, as suggested above, no national history textbooks, museum displays, or other prominent sources of public knowledge existed to inform the nation about the nineteenth- and twentieth-century migrations of Orthodox Christians from rural Bethlehem to El Salvador, or the subsequent history and experiences of Palestinian-Salvadorans. National historiography lacks attention to the theme of Palestinian migration. Although the Palestinian population was well established by 1900, it may not have surpassed a size of 800 before World War II (Suter 2002: 32).[12] Very few academic studies exist about migrations to El Salvador from the Near East, yet we know that an unsubstantiated number of Palestinians as well as Lebanese, Syrians, and Jews migrated to El Salvador during the first half of the nineteenth century.[13] It may be impossible to have accurate population statistics regarding this group, which Salvadorans popularly refer to as "Turcos" (Turks).

The vernacular "Turco" is widely used in El Salvador to refer to immigrants and descendants from the Near East. The vernacular "Chino" (Chinese) is also commonly used in El Salvador to refer to immigrants and descendants of any Far East origin. While the use of the term "Turco" likely began when the homelands of the Near East migrants to El Salvador were part of the Ottoman Empire, the continued reference to "Turcos" even for those who arrived when the Ottoman Empire was dissolved post-1932 perpetuates a misidentification. As such, because of the inaccuracy of these two categories to identify specific and ethnic origins, they function as racializing terms. Salvadorans know a "Turco" or "Chino" when they see one. Scholarship provides very few clues about the experiences of the Chinese in El Salvador. Unlike other Latin American nations, El Salvador did not import large numbers of foreign workers. Instead of mass migration, nineteenth-century Far Eastern migration to El Salvador was characterized by the arrival of individuals on their own initiative, with most immigrants originating from southern China, in particular from Canton (Suter 2002: 33). El Salvador's small geographic territory and restricted economic opportunities likely contributed to limiting El Salvador as a destination for Chinese migration. Early migration that did occur may have been a response to economic and legal discrimination in the United States, Canada, and Mexico. Later migration, in the early twentieth century, seems to have coincided with the displacement of workers after the completion of the Panama Canal.

As El Salvador attempted to modernize and consolidate a national identity in the 1930s in the aftermath of the great economic depression (Wilson 1970), there were early state-led efforts to represent a mestizo nation. Immigrant groups from the Near and Far East, including Palestinians and Chinese, though relatively small in population size, were pitted as outsiders against early twentieth-century constructions of national belonging. Xenophobic anti-immigrant attitudes grouped Palestinians together with Chinese as "pernicious" and harmful aliens (Suter 2002). Anti-foreigner (*extranjero*) and specifically anti-Chinese laws were enforced.[14] The discriminatory attitudes existed alongside other attitudes and practices that, while celebrating the indigenous roots for mestizaje, viewed contemporary indigenous populations as obstacles to national goals of progress and modernization. Thus in the early history of El Salvador's nation-building we see Palestinians, Chinese, Blacks, and Indians all marginalized in ideas of national belonging.

Although early national censuses did count Asiaticos, Palestinos, and Turcos though not in a consistent fashion, in post–civil war El Salvador census efforts did not differentiate Salvadorans in terms of race and ethnicity (except for a problematic effort to enumerate the contemporary indigenous population, discussed in the next chapter). It was, therefore, difficult for me to know the size and status of racial and ethnic communities in El Salvador. It is obvious that much research remains to be completed on El Salvador's history of immigration and ethnic studies. There is a need for research on topics such as historical national immigration policy, census technologies, individual biographies and collective histories of arrival and reception, the maintenance of ethnic community ties, and how current ethnic communities remain vibrant. My research, while underscoring particular state-led strategies to represent the nation, also serves to index the silences that continue about El Salvador's ethnic and racial history and present-day diversity.

As suggested above, archaeology was actively involved in post-war projects, particularly when it came to highlighting indigenous cultural roots. Spain's cultural influences on El Salvador were also showcased through archaeology via new excavations at the historical site of Ciudad Vieja. In 2000 CONCULTURA began reconstruction of Ciudad Vieja. Established as San Salvador in 1528, it was Spain's administrative center for the colonial territory. The site was abandoned in 1541 when its population resettled in San Salvador's present-day location. Revealed by archaeological evidence and historical documentation, the boundaries of the colonial center have now re-emerged on the landscape. Archaeologist William Fowler's research has revealed the colonial presence of multiethnic, multinational indigenous populations, including Nahuat Pipils, Tlaxcaltecs, Tetzcocans, Huexotzincans, Tepeyacans, Mexicas, Mixtecs, Soconusco Nahuas, and Kaqchikel Mayas (Fowler and Gallardo 2002). For those who wanted to promote Spain's influence on El Salvador, the site had special importance.

That Indian and Spanish cultural heritage became the two focal points for postwar nation-building projects made sense, considering that over 80 percent of El Salvador's national population probably have this mixed ancestry and therefore tend to be counted as mestizo (mixed). Mestizaje, however, is an ideology that claims that the fusion of Spaniards and Indians created a unique race. It is emblematized in José Vasconcelos's 1925 *The Cosmic Race* (*La Raza Cósmica*), a treatise on Mexican national identity. Mestizaje was the subtext for state-led efforts in postwar El Salvador that represented national society as homogeneous and mestizo. In the mestizo nation, the claims of contemporary indigenous populations were scrutinized precisely for the ability to challenge the unitary identity of national society. This model of nation-building, while celebrating ancient indigenous pasts, not only preferred, but also actually assumed as a fait accompli, the assimilation of indigenous difference into the modern national norm. The mestizo nation also neglected to reference African influences that accompanied Spanish colonization, as well as the modern migrations from the Near East, the Far East, Western Europe, and elsewhere. By defining the nation in narrow terms of mestizo identity, the government of El Salvador, scholars, media, and others misrepresented the history and full diversity of Salvadoran society.

As mentioned above, as early as the 1920s–1930s, the ideology of mestizaje was promoted as the basis of national belonging in El Salvador. It was, however, simultaneously linked to the dismantling of communal indigenous landholdings. Powerful interests deemed the land redistribution as necessary to advance the commercial expansion of crops such as coffee. Early promotions of mestizaje were also connected to efforts to eliminate indigenous culture. Working to advance goals of modernity and progress, state and society in El Salvador (as in other Latin American nations during this period) regarded indigenous difference as an obstacle to be eradicated (Gould and Lauria-Santiago 2008). Over the decades, these state policies and predominant social attitudes left a deep scar on the nation by promoting social inequality and profoundly affecting the status of El Salvador's indigenous populations while also reinforcing the exclusion of other ethnic and racial minorities.

Many nations are built around a sense of a shared national past. Anthropologists (in particular archaeologists) and historians contribute to the process of meaning-making that informs nation-building projects. As I have illustrated above, in El Salvador, emphasizing pastness was one strategy of postwar nation-building. El Salvador's unique cultural history was signified primarily as ancient indigenous heritage blended with historical Spanish influences. As I note, these particular promotions of the past also serve as a registry of silences and exclusions. In post–civil war El Salvador, however, twenty-first-century nation-building in a global context motivated the state to begin to officially recognize its contemporary indigenous population, while international supporters rallied to defend them. How the postwar nation-state newly engaged indigenous populations and subaltern claims of indigeneity, thereby expanding the meaning of national belonging, is the topic of the next chapter.

3

Envisioning Indigenous Participation

State Ambivalence, Local Activism, and International Influences

POSTWAR EFFORTS TO DEFINE El Salvador's national uniqueness emphasized archaeological and historical pasts. These new projects, some of which I described in the previous chapter, valorized pre-Columbian and historical indigenous heritage for a purportedly culturally homogeneous contemporary nation. The Salvadoran public responded in diverse ways to this approach to national culture and identity, ranging from the embrace of indigenous ancestry to ambivalence and even rejection of any such inheritance. Regardless of the public's response and the goals of the state, nation-building projects that promoted El Salvador's indigenous past perforce brought attention to the present-day status of El Salvador's indigenous Lenca, Nahuat, Cacaopera, and Maya populations. While most state-led promotions continued to relegate El Salvador's indigenous populations to the past by ignoring present-day concerns, I watched native minorities organize to demand recognition and representation, and noted how sympathies and alliances both within and outside El Salvador bolstered their efforts.

This chapter discusses postwar engagements between UN entities, the state, and indigenous organizations and populations in El Salvador. The participation of UN entities illustrates the global context of contemporary nation-building. In chapter 1 I criticized the UNESCO Culture of Peace Program for trying to create sameness across national borders by introducing a values project that was interchangeable from one postconflict nation to another, and for promoting individualism that served the logic of neoliberalism. However, UN interventions in postwar El Salvador were also about long-standing UN campaigns to articulate and defend human rights, including the collective rights of indigenous people. I will explore the tension that I observed between the ways the UN, a global agency, attempted to produce sameness and support differentiation.

This chapter is also about the tension and ambivalence in new state-led practices in El Salvador toward indigenous populations as the slow shift is made from denying the presence of El Salvador's indigenous ethnic minorities to recognizing and engaging them. In the postwar period the state established a government office to specifically address indigenous peoples' issues and began to create new policy to address Indian and nation-state relations.[1] The process was emergent and uneven, and certain policies and practices continued to marginalize native populations. State practices simultaneously recognized anew yet continued to minimize the importance of native people vis-à-vis national society. Below I explore why the state is taking a new interest in indigenous populations after decades that sought to define national belonging by absorbing indigenous cultural difference. This chapter is about the dynamics of Indian and nation-state relations, and how including Indians in ideas about the postwar nation is a vital facet of postwar nation-building in a global context.

El Salvador is not unique among nation-states grappling with tensions of race, ethnicity, and nation. The ability to recognize and celebrate social and cultural diversity is a pressing problem for many societies today. However, descendants of original and colonized populations can make particular claims on states that other minority groups cannot. The recent decades have seen increased international efforts in defense of the world's indigenous populations. The UN has played a pivotal role in creating forums to examine the effects of racial discrimination on the social and economic situation of indigenous people. Coinciding with UN attention to postwar El Salvador was the quincentenary of 1492, a historic commemoration that raised regional and international awareness about contemporary indigenous peoples worldwide. The UN had declared 1995–2004 the "International Decade of Indigenous People." This designation influenced the funding and program priorities of international governments and nongovernmental organizations that supported postwar El Salvador. Also helping to draw attention to the status of El Salvador's indigenous populations were post–civil war democratic openings that enabled Indians to publicly challenge ongoing discrimination and exclusion more safely than they had been able to in the past. The post–civil war state slowly responded to these external and internal dynamics to address its indigenous ethnic minority populations.

Brief Cultural History

In postwar El Salvador some nation-builders looked to the region's ancient past for clues about national history, culture, and identity in order to represent a unique and primordial cultural core. Their projects recognized that for centuries the territory of present-day El Salvador was a frontier zone, where heterogeneous indigenous nations likely co-existed. This did not prevent projects from focusing on a Maya heritage for postwar El Salvador (see chapter 2). While there are tremendous gaps in scholarship about the region's deep past, archaeologists suggest that the principal inhabitants were Maya-related Pokomon and Chorti, Lenca, and Xinca. Later, between 900 and 1300 CE, Nahuat speakers (identified as Pipiles in later Spanish colonial documents) migrated to the region from Central Mexico. By the sixteenth century, the Nahuat speakers dominated the cultural and political landscape of the territory they named Cuscatlán (Land of Precious Jewels or Riches). The accepted history is that the region experienced widespread interaction between the arriving Spanish, enslaved African, and indigenous populations.[2] By the early eighteenth century, it appears that the majority of the local population in El Salvador spoke Spanish, and many indigenous people had become laborers in the production and export of indigo and the fiber henequen. These early exports ushered El Salvador into a growing world economy.

In 1838 El Salvador emerged as a sovereign republic after years of struggle for territorial independence, first from Spain, then from failed early nineteenth-century attempts at a Central American federation. As they attempted to consolidate national population and territory, how did the nation-state founders contend with indigenous populations? The influences of Western Europe and emerging nation-state models were the primary inspiration for El Salvador's first patriots (Turcios 1995). In the new republic of El Salvador, it was the right of citizenship that foremost defined national belonging, and not an emphasis on indigenous cultural legacies. The extension of limited citizenship rights had analogues in the new nation-states of Western Europe and the United States. In the nineteenth century, El Salvador not only looked to European models of nation-state formation, but also Western ideas of modernity and the transforming power of progress. This paradigmatic thinking considered indigenous bodies and cultures superfluous impediments and obstacles to national goals. Although there was race mixing from earliest contact through colonialism, by the end of the nineteenth century most Salvadorans were racially mixed. National leaders pushed society toward modernization, and some indigenous elements, such as closed corporate communities and landholdings, were forcibly abandoned along the way.

I conducted research in El Salvador at the national library, perusing books, theses, journals, gazettes, and newspapers on file to compare how the nation-state was defined and represented over the years, especially the nascent years. I found very little material focused on El Salvador's ethno-racial diversity. Such an omission in key representations of the nation might suggest the social, political, and economic forces that marginalized, thus threatening, the well-being of indigenous communities. Pressures to acculturate were great. Over the decades various levels of state action and policy reinforced the popular idea that El Salvador lacked an indigenous population. Two actions had particular effect, the legacies of a 1932 state-sanctioned episode of violence against Nahuat populations and the failure of census technologies to officially record the presence of indigenous minorities. During the course of my research, I observed how the causes and consequences of 1932 were re-examined, and how the national census tried to enumerate El Salvador's indigenous population but faltered.

In 1932 there was a popular insurrection in western El Salvador wherein indigenous people and others attacked businesses and took over local government offices. The state response was swift and brutal. Many thousands of Nahuat men, women, and children were massacred over a period of weeks. The state-sanctioned violence is referred to in scholarship and in the vernacular as the Matanza (the Slaughter). The popular insurrection that preceded the Matanza took place in Sonsonate, a rural and predominantly indigenous Nahuat region of El Salvador. The insurrection was connected to early twentieth-century popular movements in El Salvador involving labor unions and urban, rural, and indigenous populations who were experiencing a lack of democracy, worker exploitation, and the dispossession of indigenous peoples and peasants from the land. The shared social and economic conditions of multiple actors were inflected with indigenous ethnicity, anti-Indian racism, class factions, gender ideologies, rural-urban distinctions, and the arrival and localization of Marxism-Leninism (Gould and Lauria-Santiago 2008). Social and political movements emerged that linked interests in predominantly indigenous rural western El Salvador to those of workers in urban San Salvador, leading to broad-based union mobilizations, strikes, rebellion, and insurgency.[3]

Due in part to the scarcity of research and evidence, the exact number of victims of the 1932 Matanza is unknown, but estimates range from 10,000 to 40,000 (T. Anderson 2001; Gould and Lauria-Santiago 2008). Jeffrey Gould and Aldo Lauria-Santiago, who characterize the violence as genocide, say their historical research cannot confirm more than 10,000 victims. However, in 2010 while making the historical apology to indigenous populations for the 1932 violence, President Mauricio Funes referred to 32,000 victims (el-salvador.com 2010). Existing written accounts, photographs, and testimonials depict groups of people being rounded up, shot, and thrown into mass graves or piled into roadside ditches. Over the years in El Salvador, interpretations and memories of the violence were mobilized by the powerful Right, as well as the Left, who used their historical interpretation of the Matanza for their own version of national history (Lindo-Fuentes, Ching, and Lara-Martínez 2007). Interpretations were associated with prevailing Cold War ideologies for both pro- and anti-Communist discourse and mobilizations, and the event was primarily linked to the potential influence of international communism in El Salvador at that time. Until recently, these interpretations of the Matanza obscured indigenous peoples' concerns as factors that motivated the 1932 popular uprising, although all recognized that Indians were the primary victims of the resulting mass violence. In the postwar period, new scholarship calls attention to the separate and unique concerns and interests of indigenous people that led up to the Matanza.[4]

It is rarely noted that the 1932 popular uprising was one of a long history of indigenous uprisings in El Salvador. Virginia Q. Tilley (2005) lists forty-three indigenous revolts that occurred between 1771 and 1918 in El Salvador. Despite a history of resistance and struggle, prior to the Matanza there was already evidence in El Salvador of the abandonment of indigenous language, attire, and other ethnic markers. In the late nineteenth century, the state actively dispossessed peasant communities in favor of commercial agriculture. This included the privatization of communal indigenous lands. Historian Lauria-Santiago (1999) examines how different indigenous communities responded to liberal efforts to make them individual entrepreneurs. Erosion to indigenous identity and well-being resulted from loss of land, impoverished living conditions, and increasing political and economic control by nonindigenous social actors, as well as overall increased interaction with nonindigenous people. That being said, the state's response in the aftermath of 1932 had a further devastating impact on the survival of indigenous people. Following the Matanza, state policies promoted ideas of a culturally homogeneous mestizo nation. In addition, leaders of indigenous communities told me that following the Matanza, older Indians' fear and the younger generation's shame about being Indian contributed to the vanishing of public expressions of indigeneity. Many outward cultural markers such as language, dress, and collective organizing disappeared. From 1932 forward the social, political, and economic marginalization of indigenous people in El Salvador persisted, and they lacked meaningful participation in national society. This dramatically reduced indigenous agency, ethnic mobilizations, and their pursuit of autonomy.

It also contributed to popular misconceptions that 1932 eliminated indigenous people from El Salvador. (One major contradiction I discovered in El Salvador is that while people will tell you there are no longer indigenous people, they will point to towns like Panchimalco, Izalco, Sonsonate, and others, as places where indigenous people still live. My research assures me that indigenous communities do indeed exist in El Salvador today.)

Today it can be difficult to identify who is an indigenous person in El Salvador, if the criteria involve public demonstrations of traditional dress,[5] spoken language, or biological "purity." While these criteria may not be readily visible to the general public, neither should they be the sole defining features of indigeneity. Native American scholars such as Eva Garoutte (2003) examine how certain definitions of who is an Indian can limit membership and identification to the detriment of indigenous peoples' future population strength and well-being. For example, definitions that are based on blood quanta can discriminate against mixed-race people. Other definitions that mandate traditional cultural expression may not take into account the decades of pressure upon native communities and their cultural practices, including the propensity today to migrate far from traditional homelands. Definitions requiring purity and tradition can constrain indigenous people and do not reflect the myriad ways that history, memory, colonization, and culture influence indigeneity today throughout the world (Starn and de la Cadena 2007).

Despite astounding pressure, indigenous communities continue to survive in El Salvador. They are among the most impoverished and marginalized populations in the nation. Due in large part to the abandonment of obvious ethnic markers and narrow definitions of authenticity, to many outsiders they may not appear to be indigenous people. As democratic apertures and global influences in postwar El Salvador permit and inspire greater public and collective expressions of indigeneity, indigenous political and cultural organizations have also expanded (Tilley 2005). While indigeneity is not new to El Salvador, the repressive national history, past trends of assimilation, and the force of official representations of mestizaje mean that some in El Salvador today view expressions of "indigenousness" as ethnogenesis, the new construction of ethnic identity, instead of cultural continuity. However, as anthropologist Henrik Ronsbo explores for the Nahuat community of Santo Domingo in western El Salvador, identity practices involve "a process whereby relations between particular signs and embodied practices are being reworked while accommodated to the emerging ethnodiscourse" wherein "'indigenousness' is part of an on-going argument over what marks the borders of the community within particular contexts" (2004: 215). In my experience, the foremost identity among indigenous people in El Salvador is to their geographical community rather than to an indigenous tribe or nation. In 2000 I was in a remote, rural community in western El Salvador that to my assessment was indigenous. Yet in conversation with the local leaders about whether they were organizing and representing themselves as such, the response was "No, not yet." This illustrates for me a fluid and dynamic process where indigenous identity is finding greater saliency and expression.

Over the decades, the national census has contributed to the notion that indigenous populations are negligible. In 1930 the national census registered 5–6 percent of the population indigenous, contradicting local birth records (Ching and Tilly 1998). At the beginning of the twenty-first century an accurate census of indigenous populations is still unavailable. This is due to the fact that for decades the national census has either neglected to count them or has performed a gross undercount. In the absence of firm statistics, scholars and others estimate the indigenous populations of Nahuat, Lenca, Cacaopera, and Maya to be approximately 500,000 or roughly 10 percent of the national population (Chapin 1989, 1990; Gobierno de El Salvador Ministerio de Salud Pública y Asistencia Social, Consejo Coordinador Nacional Indígena Salvadoreno, Organización Panamericana de la Salud 2001). It is difficult to ascertain how this number is derived, but it surely recognizes that, despite the absence of cultural markers like spoken language and traditional dress, there is a prevalence of indigenous bodies (biologically speaking) and evidence of a range of other indigenous cultural practices throughout the nation. Worldview or cosmovision, orientation to community, connection to place and environment, and traditional medicine are listed among the characteristics that organizations and agencies apply to their definition of who is indigenous. And, more often than not, it is the extreme conditions of poverty that mark who is or who is not an Indian.

The census is a powerful state technology that shapes definitions of national belonging (Kertzer and Arel 2002). Discrete categorization of national populations by race, ethnicity, language, and so forth is a political act that also brings social consequences. Similarly, the failure to recognize and account for categories of difference brings consequences as well. Whether the intended policy is national inclusion or exclusion, the census can facilitate both processes. In El Salvador the category of Indian (Indio or *natural*) was eliminated from the national census in 1940 in the aftermath of the state-sanctioned violence of 1932. The absence of indigenous people from national population statistics fed into other policies that sought to eliminate indigenous difference, and that influenced common understandings about the vanishing of native populations. Recent scholarship challenges the presumed disappearance of native populations. For example, Erik Ching and Virginia Tilley (1998) compared post-1932 national population statistics to local birth registry statistics and noted that native births were recorded in local registries even when the national census eliminated the data.

In the postwar period, largely in response to the gap in official data about indigenous populations, the Pan American Health Organization, the international public health agency affiliated with the World Health Organization, worked with El Salvador's Ministry of Public Health and Social Assistance and with Consejo Coordinador Nacional Indígena Salvadoreña (CCNIS), an umbrella indigenous organization formed after the civil war, to sponsor and collect census and other population information from three indigenous communities in western El Salvador: Cuisnahut, Izalco, and Nahuizalco. Their efforts to understand contemporary indigenous populations revealed the contradictions between local- and state-level priorities, and also juxtaposed state-level inattention to international interest in the well-being of El Salvador's indigenous ethnic minorities. The internationally sponsored research was an important acknowledgment of the presence of contemporary indigenous populations in El Salvador. The resulting publication offered census-like data on the health status of indigenous communities (Gobierno de El Salvador Ministerio de Salud Pública y Asistencia Social, Consejo Coordinador Nacional Indígena Salvadoreno, Organización Panamericana de la Salud 2001). Providing documentation of their difficult living conditions was critical for pressuring the state to do more to support this neglected population.

More than a tool for domestic audiences, the national census is also a required practice for participation in the international community of nation-states. The way the census does or does not represent national populations can raise the attention of international suprastate governing bodies such as the UN. During the postwar period, El Salvador's census practices and other policies affecting indigenous ethnic minority populations reached the UN Committee on the Elimination of Racial Discrimination (UNCERD). On May 19, 2005, the government of El Salvador submitted a tardy report to the UNCERD explaining why the government had missed five requested reports to the agency for the years 1996, 1998, 2000, 2002, and 2004. The gaps in reporting were blamed on civil war recovery, and on the debilitating natural disasters of hurricanes and earthquakes. The report that was finally presented to the UNCERD was replete with contradictions about the status of indigenous populations.[6]

The report claimed that, on one hand, El Salvador has a negligible indigenous population, and on the other hand, that it had engaged in new efforts to address its indigenous population, such as establishing the Office of Indigenous Affairs (discussed below), and that it intended to develop a national politica indígena. The report stated, however, that because the indigenous population is dispersed throughout Salvadoran society, racism does not exist in the country; therefore no special legislation was necessary to protect the rights of indigenous people. Further, the report affirmed that despite the urging of El Salvador's indigenous organizations, and even international pressure to do so, El Salvador would not ratify the International Labor Organization's Convention 169 that recognizes the cultural rights of indigenous and tribal peoples.[7] The rationale for not signing onto the international convention was that doing so would violate the equal rights provision in El Salvador's national constitution. Also by citing a general amnesty law that impedes investigation or compensation for certain situations, the official delegation representing the government of El Salvador rejected the idea of providing any moral or economic recognition for indigenous people who survived

1932 or other episodes of state violence. The state's stance against adopting certain policies on behalf of indigenous people points to the tension between international understandings and expectations and nation-state practices.

Anticipating that the government would continue its reluctance to commit fully to policies or actions to address the well-being of its indigenous ethnic minority, a coalition of human rights and social justice organizations in El Salvador presented the UNCERD with a separate "shadow report" (Federación Luterana Mundial 2005). The report summarized relevant recent research and other sources of information depicting the contemporary conditions and continued marginalization of El Salvador's indigenous populations.[8] The broad coalition of social actors involved in the shadow report demonstrated that there was increasing civil society support for indigenous people in El Salvador. UNCERD responded to the shadow report by calling attention to the government of El Salvador's ambivalent policies and contradictory positions.

In 2007, partly in response to international pressure and to demonstrate follow-through in developing an Indian policy, El Salvador's national census attempted to gauge the size and whereabouts of its indigenous population. The result, however, was a disastrous undercounting. Of a national population of 5,744,113, the census counted just 0.2 percent as indigenous. This stands in contrast to the unofficial figure of 10 percent commonly cited by indigenous organizations in El Salvador, UN agencies, and so on. The undercount was blamed in part on methodology. The census did not allow for self-identification, so instead census takers made judgments about who was or was not indigenous. Other than the census takers' subjective view, no official criteria were applied. (In Mexico, for example, the census uses "speaks an indigenous language" as a criterion. Due to the very low number of fluent speakers of indigenous languages in El Salvador, this approach would have resulted in an even more miniscule census figure for El Salvador's indigenous ethnic minorities.) Allowing self-identification could have had some effect on increasing the numbers, at least according to some members of indigenous communities in western El Salvador. However, given the history of repression and ongoing discrimination in El Salvador, and considering that many indigenous people in Latin America (and elsewhere) define their identities in other ways or keep their indigenousness to themselves, the assumption that the national census is able to provide an accurate statistic is questionable. Anthropologists and other scholars examining contemporary indigenous identity tend to emphasize a more historical and processual view of indigenous identity, and recognize its relationship to cultural survival and to resistance (Field 1994; Starn and de la Cadena 2007).

On May 28, 2008, Miguel Huezo Mixco, a noted Salvadoran culture critic and national cultural policy consultant, published a scathing essay in the daily newspaper *La Prensa Gráfica* entitled "El Salvador: The Census Erased Indians Off the Map."

> What occurred with the census and the Indians is more than a technical error. Now they are more invisible . . . less subject to rights, less citizens. Nobody wants to magnify the size of this population. The Indians are a minority, but it is precisely due to this condition that the State has an obligation to protect their political, economic, cultural, and human rights. These are not privileges, but rights. And it is not an act of charity, but a contribution to the democracy and the stability of the country."[9] (Translation mine.)

The commentary represented the viewpoints of many in El Salvador who advocated not only on behalf of indigenous people but who saw the continued denial of El Salvador's indigenous ethnic minority as a blight on efforts to restore humanity to postwar society.

Some activists have requested that the new census figures not be allowed to stand as an official representation of El Salvador's minority population, but appeals to the national Corte Suprema de Justicia to annul the census figures were not acknowledged. In my discussions with government officials in El Salvador about what might be done to achieve a more accurate census, they reminded me of the exorbitant price tag associated with any national census effort. They suggested to me that a renewed effort to provide better census figures was not on the near horizon. While the faulty census is a disappointment and a missed opportunity, other state efforts did engage El Salvador's indigenous population.

The Office of Indigenous Affairs

In 1995 the postwar government established the Office of Indigenous Affairs (Asuntos Indígenas) as an early demonstration to the international community that it was connecting with indigenous populations. Until 2009 Indigenous Affairs was administered by CONCULTURA under the auspices of the Ministry of Education. Today it is handled by the newly established Secretariat of Culture, under the program Social Inclusion. I have engaged with the staff of Indigenous Affairs from its early existence while it was under the direction of respected Salvadoran anthropologist Gloria Aracely Gutierrez de Mejía. It was always a small operation with one or two staff members. After Gutierrez de Mejía's untimely death from illness, her assistant Rita Ercilia Araujo was put in charge of the unit. We have maintained steady contact over the years.

The Office of Indigenous Affairs was created after a series of postwar government projects by CONCULTURA to record and rescue indigenous language and culture. CONCULTURA was collecting folkloric or traditional indigenous expressive practices widely viewed as about to completely disappear from the national landscape. As state programs sought symbols of the unique nation, they looked foremost to forms of indigenous expression. Popular folktales, such as the *Siguanaba*, and dances, such as the *Tiger and the Deer* (*El Tigre y El Venado*), revealed El Salvador's indigenous roots. CONCULTURA set out to record indigenous cultural practices and promote certain projects to reinforce cultural traditions. One CONCULTURA project instituted the teaching of Nahuat language in sixteen primary schools in western El Salvador. The project was presented in 1992 at the first Congreso Linguistico del Idioma Nahuat, a scholarly symposium about the Nahuat language organized by CONCULTURA. To the national and international scholars in attendance, CONCULTURA stated that future efforts would go beyond the technical study of Nahuat language to include the identification of existing native language speakers. In 1994, at the second Congreso Linguistico del Idioma Nahuat, Nahuat-speaking members of local indigenous communities were also in attendance. Following that symposium, CONCULTURA decided to expand the narrow focus on Nahuat language to work more directly with indigenous communities in El Salvador.

These events occurred in the early years of the postwar peace accords when international presence and contributions to postwar nation-building were at their zenith, and when the UN had declared the International Decade of the World's Indigenous Peoples. This is the juncture and context that surrounded the establishment of El Salvador's governmental Office of Indigenous Affairs. Indigenous Affairs states that its mission is to "serve and support indigenous populations, communities, and organizations in all of their manifestations in benefit of National Cultural Identity."[10] This objective suggests a delicate balancing act. Indigenous Affairs is at once an advocate for the interests of indigenous people and is an extension of the Salvadoran government. High-level staffers from CONCULTURA and Indigenous Affairs attend international forums as representatives of El Salvador's indigenous populations. Indigenous Affairs makes political alliances with some indigenous communities and organizations, but not others. Some in the indigenous peoples' movement blame Indigenous Affairs for creating divisions between communities and exacerbating tensions over limited resources. Nonetheless, the existence of Indigenous Affairs communicated the state's desire to engage indigenous populations.

In July 2009 I visited Indigenous Affairs. Rita Ercilia Araujo proudly handed me the glossy pamphlet "Indigenous Population and Intercultural Education in El Salvador" (Población Indígena y Educación Intercultural en El Salvador). The pamphlet described the state's goal to recognize indigenous populations and promote tolerance and cultural understanding toward them throughout the nation. The pamphlet included relevant references to clauses from the national constitution, the Universal Declaration of Human Rights, and UNICEF's Convention on the Rights of the Child. This illustrated the UN's influence on new national programs and policies. The pamphlet also provided useful information about El Salvador's indigenous populations. There was a listing of sixty municipalities with indigenous populations, and information on select indigenous concepts, worldviews, traditional cultural practices, and characteristics of indigenous people in El Salvador. The overriding message was that indigenous people exist and are to be recognized as indigenous ethnic minorities but also as Salvadorans. A direct representation of this status was found in the pamphlet's translation of El Salvador's national hymn into Nahuat ("Takwikalis Tutal" or "Canto a Nuestra Tierra"). Here we return full circle to the early postwar efforts, when the priority to record and rescue indigenous language and cultural practices was motivated by the search for symbols of the unique nation. Contemporary indigenous people could symbolize the unique nation. It remains to be seen what additional state policies will follow and whether they will result in the improved status of native populations.

As described above, the state is engaged with international entities, such as UN agencies, in efforts to provide indigenous populations with a meaningful place in Salvadoran society. International attention to indigenous people in El Salvador placed expectations on the nation-state to acknowledge their rights. The attention and expectations also informed international social and economic development investments in El Salvador. In postwar El Salvador, the state's recent and still-incipient recognition of its indigenous ethnic minority population can appear motivated by the international resources that rewarded state efforts to address indigenous populations. Just as chapter 1 traced the influence of UNESCO's Culture of Peace Program on state educational policies, it is possible to look at the international factors that stimulated nation-state attention to indigenous populations. They represent a twenty-first-century global context for nation-building and how it influences the remaking of the meaning of national belonging.

The UN declared 1992–2001 the International Decade of the World's Indigenous Peoples and 2001–2010 the International Decade for the Culture of Peace and Non-Violence for the Children of the World. In the aftermath of El Salvador's civil war, these themes became charters that influenced certain international social and economic investments in El Salvador. The few funded activities from the Culture of Peace Program proposal discussed in chapter 1 were those that promoted the protection of human rights, with particular attention to the rights of women, children, and indigenous people. In addition, the Values Program based on the Culture of Peace proposal emphasized civic values of "social coexistence," "respect for others," and "cultural identity," all conceivably connected with shaping meanings to support El Salvador's indigenous minority population.

During my fieldwork I observed the emergence of similar and related internationally sponsored projects. In January 2000,

UNICEF–El Salvador received funds from a UNICEF support branch in the United States for "Project Maya." The funds were earmarked for projects concerning children's health and education, in particular for exploratory research on the demographics of El Salvador's indigenous populations. Although named "Project Maya," there was no requirement that the project exclusively serve populations that identified as such. In 2000 Vicente Gavidia, El Salvador's UNICEF coordinator, asked me to provide him with information about El Salvador's indigenous populations. Did indigenous populations really exist here, and where? And which communities should his office work with? Were they Maya? Gavidia was not only unsure of the whereabouts of native communities, but whether Maya would be their accurate ethnic attribution. In earlier chapters I explored how "Maya" serves as a metonym for diverse indigenous communities in El Salvador as well as a reference to historical and contemporary connections certain groups have with Maya communities in nearby Guatemala and Honduras. Some indigenous groups today attach "Maya" to a hyphenated cultural affiliation, for example "Lenca-Maya" or "Nahuat-Maya." Contemporary cultural exchanges also strengthen links between Maya and indigenous Salvadoran populations. For example, I have participated in ritual ceremonies in El Salvador led by Maya cultural experts from Guatemala.[11] As an umbrella term, Maya offered name recognition that served indigenous organizations as well as state tourism development projects and has facilitated El Salvador's participation in regional projects such as Mundo Maya and Ruta Maya. Because Gavidia was accustomed to providing national population data that was undifferentiated by race or ethnicity, he was surprised about the project's interest in this particular subgroup. His surprise applied as much to UNICEF's Project Maya as to my own interest in the status of indigenous people in postwar El Salvador.

Dr. Edgardo Platero, a Salvadoran medical professional who worked with the El Salvador branch of the Pan American Health Organization, a division of the World Health Organization, was one person who did not need to be convinced about the presence and status of El Salvador's indigenous populations. He had directed the partnership between the Ministry of Public Health and Social Assistance and CCNIS to research the basic health conditions in six indigenous communities (discussed above). He told me that the increase in international attention to the needs of indigenous populations in El Salvador was tied to regional development projects that used Mexico and Guatemala as models for projects in smaller nation-states such as El Salvador. Because Mexico and Guatemala had sizeable indigenous populations, the assumption was made that El Salvador also has indigenous populations, even when the nation-state was reluctant to acknowledge the fact.

During field research in El Salvador, I learned that a number of new development projects were requiring the government of El Salvador to demonstrate whether the projects would affect indigenous communities. In 2000 I was invited to meet with officials in the Ministry of Agriculture and Livestock about El Salvador's participation in the Unidad Regional de Asistencia Técnica (RUTA), a Central American regional agriculture and cattle development project overseen by the UN Development Program, with funding from the World Bank and cooperation from the International Development Bank, the Inter-American Institute for Cooperation on Agriculture, the Food and Agriculture Organization of the United Nations, and the International Fund for Agricultural Development, in addition to contributions from governments of the United Kingdom, Denmark, Japan, Norway, and Sweden. One basic criterion for nation-state participation in RUTA was that national governments had a politica indígena and mechanisms for engaging indigenous populations that may be affected by development in the region. Requiring the nation-state to recognize indigenous populations as a basis for participation in internationally funded development projects presented an interesting challenge for El Salvador's government that had previously represented the nation as devoid of such a population, or at best had been ambivalent about the place in national society for native populations. The international expectations challenged El Salvador's past efforts to absorb its indigenous population, its current indecisive stance, and lack of national policy, and motivated the state to begin to recognize its indigenous population as never before. As the government moved closer to developing a national Indian policy, largely in response to this international and local pressure, Indigenous Affairs served as the primary intermediary between indigenous organizations and communities, and the state.

One way to explain why the state has taken new interest in its indigenous populations after decades of seeking to define national belonging by absorbing indigenous cultural difference is that it is responding to international expectations. When El Salvador's postwar government asserted its commitment to supporting a democratic postwar society, it also began to acknowledge its contemporary indigenous populations. There were potential political and economic gains for doing so that improved El Salvador's standing in the international community. In addition to the external motivation, there was internal motivation. The indigenous political movement in El Salvador had grown steadily during the postwar period (Tilley 2005). It, too, was supported by international organizations such as the UN, regional and global networking of indigenous peoples, and diasporic Salvadorans who defined their connection to El Salvador primarily through expressions of indigeneity (DeLugan forthcoming). Further, as described in this chapter, members of Salvadoran society, including academics, activists, and those in popular media, contributed new scholarship and practices that highlighted the place of indigenous people in the nation's history and society, and that challenged official representations. This dynamic contemporary context motivated the state to begin to revise past policies and practices toward indigenous populations and to fundamentally expand the meaning of national belonging.

The changing status of indigenous people in El Salvador, motivated by international actors and other global dynamics, mirrors similar actions in other Latin American nation-states where indigenous people are becoming "new" citizens and/or gaining new rights and recognition.[12] With their newly defined citizenship often coming in the form of individual rights, indigenous people are vulnerable to co-optation, and autonomous indigenous representation may be threatened. Further, in a now classic essay, Charles Hale (2002) examined the convergence of neoliberal economic policy, multiculturalism, and the ways that indigenous people are becoming "new" national subjects. Critics, such as Hale, point to neoliberalism's and globalization's need for difference, that is, the cultural logic of postmodernity, and see a menacing process that fragments society based on race/ethnicity to achieve capitalistic development, market access to new lands and resource extraction, and to produce new cultural commodities.

Further, Hale draws attention to the limits of the state's new efforts to recognize multiculturalism. Focusing only on cultural recognition does little to improve the material conditions or political rights of indigenous people. While conducting fieldwork in western Sonsonate, I attended meetings with indigenous leaders who were applying for governmental and UN funding to support Nahuat language learning. As we met, I noted children who were shoeless and showed signs of malnutrition. From conversations I knew that most parents could not afford basic school materials for their children, and some could barely afford basic food. Though the population's impoverishment was dire, there did not appear to be any ready funding sources to help with basic necessities, and instead the supporters' funding priority was placed on language learning. While I understand the value of indigenous language survival as instrumental to culture, history, and identity, I also believe this illustrates Hale's critique of multiculturalism.

But what about the human rights dimension? What about the real ways that indigenous people in El Salvador understand their subordination and colonization and endeavor for the state and others to recognize and help improve their status? How do I square the critique of neoliberal multiculturalism with efforts intended to improve the lives of a marginalized population? While visiting indigenous communities and organizations in El Salvador, it was not uncommon for me to see copies of ILO Convention 169 sticking out from the back of someone's jeans pocket, or in small stacks on tables with other relevant literature. The Convention addresses issues of vital importance to the material and economic well-being of indigenous and tribal peoples, including the rights of ownership and possession over the lands they traditionally occupy or have had access to (Article 14); the rights to natural resources (Article 15); displacement (Article 16); land alienation (Article 17); unauthorized intrusions (Article 18); agrarian programs (Article 19); conditions of employment (Article 20); vocational training, handicrafts, and rural industries (Articles 21–23); social security and health (Articles 24 and 25); education (Articles 26–31); and cross-border cooperation (Article 32).[13] While it remains to be seen the extent to which this international instrument will influence improvements in El Salvador, it continues to be viewed by many indigenous leaders in El Salvador as a vehicle for recognition, increased sovereignty, and material well-being. Considering the particular nation-state context where previously there was no official recognition of El Salvador's minority ethnic indigenous population, I argue that the international expectations are creating more benefit than harm, at least at this point in time. As state-led practices develop policies and programs that begin to recognize indigenous ethnic minorities, indigenous actors also maneuver accordingly.

In 2007, after seventy-five years of fear and silence, the indigenous Nahuat from the community of Izalco (the epicenter of the 1932 violence) organized a three-day public gathering to bring attention to the historical memory of the Matanza and to the ongoing struggles of indigenous people. I attended the event along with other international supporters including Salvadorans living in the United States, representatives from human rights agencies, scholars, activists, and residents from nearby indigenous communities in western El Salvador. Some national media covered the event. At that time El Salvador's Human Rights Ombudsman (Procuradería de los Derechos Humanos) and the Human Rights Institute of the Universidad Centroamericana "José Simeón Cañas" had started to gather and examine 1932 testimonials as evidence to support a possible legal charge of genocide. Social justice activists sought recognition for the thousands of Indian bodies still buried in mass graves in western El Salvador. Others saw commemorative practices as essential to revalorizing indigenous cultural identity. These new activities rescued the 1932 violence and its effects from oblivion, while reminding post–civil war state and society about indigenous peoples' issues and concerns.

Three years later, in January 2010, the third consecutive annual public commemoration for the victims of 1932 was again held in Izalco. Attending this commemoration was an official from El Salvador's new Secretariat of Culture. The participation represented the first gesture by the state to acknowledge this dark episode of the nation's past. In October of that same year, at the occasion of El Salvador's first Congreso Nacional Indigéna, President Mauricio Funes offered an official apology for 1932 and the historical attempts to exterminate indigenous populations. Most recently, in May 2011, a delegation from the government of El Salvador participated for the first time at the tenth session of the Permanent Forum on Indigenous Issues. In their official statement they underscored the Funes administration's new attitude and vision regarding the nation's indigenous population as compared to previous administrations, restating that the traditional policy of no recognition and exclusion of indigenous peoples in El Salvador has come to an end. Here again is another hopeful indication that Indian and nation-state relations are transforming in El Salvador.

Conclusion

It can be argued that indigenous populations in El Salvador are a population confined to the margins of the territorial nation-state. Although they are the descendants of the aboriginal population and committed to native lands, they have been steadily subordinated through centuries of colonization and modern nation-building. During the civil war, the marginalization of indigenous populations was unchanged, although as outlined above, the postwar era suggests new opportunities.

International agencies influenced postwar El Salvador in ways that also supported El Salvador's indigenous populations. Whether the global expectations were linked to human rights, or to recognizing the impact of local development on indigenous minorities, the conditions are ripe in El Salvador for social identities historically repressed to find expression and re-emerge. This dynamic challenged the state's past efforts to absorb its indigenous populations and its current indecisive stance and lack of national policy, and motivated the state to recognize its indigenous populations as never before.

If indigenous people are bound to traditional lands despite nation-state negations, for them and other members of Salvadoran society the civil war created such terror and convulsion that many hundreds of thousands of Salvadorans fled national territory for survival. The out-migration that started during the civil war had continued over the years, and today a number approximating one-third of El Salvador's 6,000,000 national population live in another country. As is the case in other migrant-sending states, the national economy is now dependent on the remittances that migrants and faraway citizens send back to El Salvador, and migration serves as a safety valve that releases citizens who would otherwise struggle against limited employment opportunities. The postwar government is extremely attentive to faraway citizens. The next chapter examines how transnational state practices responded to migration and are reimagining the meaning of national belonging by including faraway citizens. Migration and transnational state practices is another vital facet that illustrates the global context of El Salvador's postwar nation-building process.

4

Remapping the Nation

Faraway Citizens,
Transnational State Practices,
and the Impact of Migration

STATE-LED PRACTICES IN postwar El Salvador focused on culture, history, and identity as a means to unite a fragmented and polarized national society. Earlier chapters described practices inspired by UNESCO to develop a culture of peace that emphasized universally accepted cultural values, and how instruction of these values has been integrated into the national educational curriculum. Another approach promoted pre-Columbian and other representations of indigenous heritage to emphasize El Salvador's unique identity. I have also shown how contemporary indigenous populations and their national and international allies criticized such practices. They complained that the state-led projects depicted native populations as existing only in the nation's past, and that the state ignored the fact that contemporary native populations exist in extreme states of poverty and lack meaningful national participation. If the state promotes indigenous heritage, they argued, it must also recognize that indigenous populations continue to exist today. Meanwhile, responding as well to international pressure, in the first decade of the twenty-first century, the state appeared poised to develop a comprehensive national Indian policy. All of the nation-building efforts described above illustrate a dynamic process of defining and redefining the meaning of national belonging.

So far I have focused on state practices directed toward El Salvador's domestic population. The domestic audience is certainly the primary audience for state-led efforts to reimagine the postwar nation. However, massive out-migration that began during the civil war and that continues apace today also motivated the state to consider faraway citizens in postwar nation-building projects. Throughout this book I have emphasized how global neoliberal policies impacted El Salvador. The macrostructural economic adjustments, such as the privatization of national resources and the introduction of cheap assembly labor for new manufacturing free trade zones, were among the postwar changes to El Salvador's economy that did not benefit most Salvadorans. Increases in the basic cost of living and the lack of employment opportunities motivated many hundreds of thousands to emigrate. In many ways, El Salvador was not very different from other developing countries. Twenty-first-century conditions in our rapidly globalizing world make migration an increasing phenomenon that affects both migrant-sending and migrant-receiving nation-states. This chapter examines how migration impacts El Salvador, and in particular how traditional state-led nation-building practices expanded to address and to connect with Salvadorans who live outside of national territory. The state developed plans to increase the participation of faraway citizens in the economic and political life of El Salvador. However, it is important to note at the outset that the state's preference for transnational participation had a class-based or economic-status dimension. Successful migrants and their progeny were wooed, while unsuccessful migrants, especially those deported back to El Salvador, were rejected. This research contributes to the increasing scholarship that examines the impact of migration on El Salvador, the growing Salvadoran diaspora, and various aspects of transnational belonging (see for example, Baker Cristales 2004; Coutin 2007, 2010; DeLugan 2008; Mixco 2009; Rivas 2007, 2010; Rodriguez 2005). How global migration and transnationalism influences nation-building is of growing interest to scholars (Brettell 2003; Schiller and Fouron 2001; Itzigsohn, 2000; Louie 2004; Smith and Bakker 2007; Smith and Guarnizo 1998; Vertovec 2009). The practices of El Salvador's postwar government provide a case study of how meanings of national belonging are reshaped in response to the global context of migration, diaspora, and transnationalism.

Currently there are an estimated two million Salvadorans abroad compared to a domestic national population of slightly less than six million. The US Census Bureau's 2005–2009 American Community Survey estimated 1,472,674 with origin from El Salvador.[1] Migrant remittances are critical to the survival of El Salvador's economy. Migrants' long-distance social, economic, and political participation, as well as the added economic stimulus provided through their short return visits to El Salvador, are the primary reasons why faraway citizens are an important focus of postwar nation-building. State practices try to reinforce the affective ties that bind emigrant *hermanos lejanos* (faraway brothers and sisters) and their descendants to El Salvador in much the same way that other state practices attempt to strengthen the ties between members of the domestic population and the nation-state. This chapter explores how new state practices innovatively reshape the meaning of national belonging by incorporating migrant and diasporic Salvadorans.

Departures, Arrivals, and the Fostering of Long-distance Ties

When a Salvadoran travels to or from El Salvador, it is cause for a major social ritual. Family and friends gather to joyfully greet or tearfully send off one of their own. For those who are traveling by air, cars and flatbed truckloads of family and friends will make a collective pilgrimage to Comalapa International Airport just southwest of the nation's capital, San Salvador. Although Comalapa is often characterized by unpredictable flight schedules and long delays, for the throngs of family and friends who gather, the airport waiting time is no bother. Instead, family members (young and old) while away the time in ad hoc family reunions. Airport time and place becomes a space where personal interactions, the sharing of memory tales, and effusive displays of care and concern reinforce kinship and other social bonds. Gift giving is an important practice of the airport ritual. It is a time-honored tradition that those arriving from distant lands bring a heavy cargo of gifts for one and for all. Clothing, electronics, toys, perfumes, and colognes are popular anticipated gifts. Those leaving El Salvador, whether for the first time or the twentieth time, will also receive gifts that serve as *recuerdos* (souvenirs and reminders) of their homeland. The most common of these mementos are T-shirts or beach towels that brandish some mark of El Salvador's uniqueness. The illustrations may include pre-Columbian imagery, reference to ecotourism sites of natural beauty, or cartoon characters spewing phrases in *caliche* (El Salvador's unique local slang which mixes Spanish and indigenous languages). Other common gifts are selections of locally made cheese, such as *petacón*, often wrapped in foil to not only appear as bullion but also seemingly treasured as such. Other frequently noted departure gifts are Café Listo—a potent instant coffee—and *quesadilla*—a typical dessert for afternoon coffee breaks.

The traveler's last meal in El Salvador is another important signifier of the familiar that will be left behind. Along the forty-minute highway ride from San Salvador to the airport is the small town of Olocuiltla. A visit here is an extension of the airport ritual. The outskirts of Olocuiltla flank both sides of the highway and are marked by the concentration of roadside *comedors* (simple, informal, open-air eateries). Here they serve *pupusas* by the hundreds. Pupusas are made of flour or rice dough and stuffed with cheese or meat before being patted into a pancake-like form and then grilled. They are El Salvador's iconic food. Many consider a stop at Olocuitla a required element of the airport pilgrimage. It functions as the "last meal" that strengthens the spirit of the sojourner, or the "welcome home" for returning Salvadorans who are nostalgic for a familiar meal. In a similar fashion, Pollo Campero serves as another gathering place for food-based airport rituals. Pollo Campero, a Guatemalan restaurant chain, is ubiquitous in El Salvador. One of the restaurants is located inside the airport. It is not unusual to see travelers preparing to pass through metal detectors on their way to board flights, only to have a bag of fried chicken from Pollo Campero thrust upon them. The gesture prompts tears from the already homesick voyagers as well as from family members being left behind. Because of this pervasive practice, flights from El Salvador often reek with the smell of fried chicken. It is a source of constant humor, as well as disdain, by some who see in it a lack of worldly sophistication.

For those emigrant sojourners who manage brief return visits home, an important landmark awaits. Upon entering San Salvador a large monument greets: Hermanos Lejanos Bienvenido (Welcome Faraway Brothers [and Sisters]). The monument was erected in 1994 by the municipal government of San Salvador as homage to the many Salvadoran patriots (*compatriotas salvadoreños*) who reside outside of national territory. This was the first monument erected during the postwar era, preceding any public statue or monument in memory of the civil war or for the victims of war.

While El Salvador has a history of emigration dating back to the nineteenth century, its magnitude was low key in comparison to the out-migration that occurred during the civil war (Cordova 2005). From the late 1970s forward, many hundreds of thousands left El Salvador. During the civil war they sought political refuge in the United States, Australia, Canada, and Europe. Out-migration continues at a rapid pace as Salvadorans today do not seek shelter from civil war, but instead are desperate for economic survival. Although the civil war ended in 1992, most of those who fled the violence are not returning home. They continue to maintain residences far away from their original homeland. Nonetheless, many make regular visits to El Salvador to return for holidays such as the annual saints' festivals held in local towns (*fiestas patronales*), Easter holy week (*semana santa*) festivities, the week-long national holiday during August (*fiestas agostinas*), or Christmas and New Year holidays. The return visits contribute to the tourist economy of El Salvador, a budding and important economic sector (Landolt, Autler, and Baires 1999).

Even if unable to make return visits, many emigrants support their families and communities through regular monetary remittances. In 2010, El Salvador's Central Bank estimated that remittances totaled $3.5 billion. This official figure represents the monetary transfers registered by the national banking system and does not include the many unofficial *maleta* (suitcase) transfers of personal goods and funds. Maleta transfers refer to the hand-delivery of cash, gifts, and greetings back and forth on behalf of oneself, or on behalf of other Salvadoran emigrants who are unable to travel to El Salvador. This vibrant social practice is now a tradition.

In the business section of the daily newspapers, the reporting of remittance levels receives the same attention as stock market prices and commodity quotes. The reporting reinforces national recognition that the emigrant is a crucial national resource. It may also explain why the first post–civil war monument in El Salvador is dedicated to Los Hermanos Lejanos. Many of El Salvador's emigrants, considered by the state to be transnational citizens, are portrayed today as national heroes.

My research followed several state-led programs that emerged to address El Salvador's emigrant population, and I explore how the meaning of national belonging was expanded in the process. In 2000, El Salvador's Ministry of Economy initiated a national Program of Competitivity, focused on enhancing El Salvador's fiscal standing. Prioritizing projects that could further national economic goals, the program identified three growth areas: the emigrant community, tourism, and arts and crafts industries. Sandra Novoa de Castillo, an official of the Ministry of Economy, and a specialist for the program's focus on the emigrant community, shared information with me about novel state-led projects to address diasporic citizens. At the time of our interview, the conservative estimate was that over one million Salvadorans lived abroad. Novoa de Castillo suggested that the real number was actually much higher. She indicated that the current estimate only counted Salvadorans who have legally emigrated from El Salvador, thus omitting the many thousands of undocumented Salvadorans abroad. Further, Novoa de Castillo insisted that we must not simply count the individuals who have emigrated from El Salvador but must include the families that these citizens create abroad. The government claims the foreign-born children of Salvadoran parents as Salvadoran citizens, and permits dual citizenship. With this expanded definition of Salvadoran nationality and attendant citizenship, and with the productive birthrates of Salvadorans (which she estimated as four plus per family on average), Novoa de Castillo calculated a whopping 4,000,000 Salvadorans that currently live abroad. (Instead of intending to represent an actual number, however, I took her message to be that the population abroad was one that is growing rapidly if not exponentially.) The largest populations of Salvadorans live in the United States, with intense concentrations in California, New York, Texas, and Washington, DC. Census efforts by the Salvadoran government to pinpoint emigrant populations are described below.

The government of El Salvador developed innovative approaches to strengthen ties between Salvadorans abroad and the nation-state. In 1999 the Ministry of the Exterior created the General Direction for Attention to Communities in the Exterior (Dirección General de Atención al Comunidades en el Exterior). In 2000 I spoke with Dr. Mario Roger Hernandez, director of the new entity. He outlined a number of government efforts, stating that a top priority was to contact strategic communities of Salvadorans in the United States, particularly communities that have already formed hometown associations. Hometown associations (*comites del pueblo*) refer to the networking of transnational emigrants who reaffirm their commitment to families and friends by investing in projects to improve the quality of life in their original home region (Paul and Gammage 2004). The Salvadoran government estimates that there are 200 hometown associations throughout the United States. A recent study estimates that 4 percent of Salvadorans in the United States have membership in a hometown association (Orozco and Garcia-Zanella 2009).[2]

Activities of hometown associations have been of great benefit to the Salvadoran government because they successfully undertake public works projects such as the building of roads, schools, parks, and other infrastructure. On the other hand, the various levels of government are often bypassed in the process of community development. According to Hernandez, this has resulted in projects being undertaken that the government did not consider the best use of funds for a particular community. The example provided to me was one project that sent an ambulance to a community that did not have a hospital, and where investments in healthcare infrastructure versus transportation would have been more timely and useful. Likewise, the government of El Salvador has been unable to provide input or to get credit for local community development advanced through these independent and privately funded public works projects. Through the new office, General Direction for Attention to Communities in the Exterior, the state proposes to assist the hometown associations by facilitating a process of donation and investment. United for Solidarity (Unidos por la Solidaridad) was a government effort developed to support and direct the contributions and activities of hometown associations. The initiative is managed by the government of El Salvador's Social Investment and Local Development

Fund. The government works to facilitate involvement of hometown associations with local development projects that include improvements related to infrastructure, recreation, and health. The state wants to enter transactions that involve the transnational transfer of resources. The government seeks a voice in decision-making about what resources are needed and how they should be invested. The government proposed that in exchange for their involvement in transnational transfer of resources, they will streamline the bureaucracy of state services while ensuring the donated resources meet the best needs of the Salvadoran communities involved. The state offers to provide an official assessment of priorities that will allow donations from those in the diaspora to be directed to meaningful local improvements and development. Through the process of hometown associations working in partnership with the government, the government contends that faraway Salvadorans might feel that they are true actors with a direct influence and impact on the future of El Salvador. The anticipated result, according to Hernandez, is that loyalties to the nation-state will be strengthened as well as a sense of belonging to El Salvador. Greater involvement of the state in the long-distance transfer of resources may be a hard sell for some Salvadorans both in the diaspora and at home. It means overcoming the mistrust of government that many Salvadorans have in common. Further, as José Itzigsohn and Daniela Villacrés (2008) describe through the example of the disbanding of one influential hometown association that was focused on development in the rural town of Intipucá, Morazan, El Salvador, not everyone benefits from hometown investments from faraway Salvadorans. This can cause inequalities to be exacerbated in the original homeland, and for suspicion and mistrust to develop both here and there.

Transnational Cultural Spaces

Beyond channeling remittance activities and forming partnerships with hometown associations, state-led projects attempt to extend the same official projects that promote postwar national culture, history, and identity to domestic audiences to faraway Salvadorans. Today the Secretariat of Culture extends projects of its previous entity

CONCULTURA. It proposes to develop "cultural spaces" in the United States for Salvadorans living there. The cultural spaces will be places where Salvadorans can gather, where there will be material about El Salvador's national culture, and where they can promote the talents of Salvadorans. Four strategic cities were initially selected: Los Angeles, Houston, Washington, DC, and New York City. The consulates in these cities are responsible for organizing the cultural spaces. Unfortunately, many Salvadorans abroad tend to have negative attitudes about the consulates. A common belief is that the consulates serve foremost a diplomatic function. In that regard, regular Salvadorans perceive them as elitist, and they have apparently been treated in ways that merit the accusation. The new mandate is for consulates to direct their attention to the needs of their local emigrant communities. The state is, therefore, trying to extend its reach to faraway citizens through improved consular services and by assigning the consulate a role in promoting Salvadoran history and culture to diasporic communities. Through new practices and the creation of spaces to promote El Salvador, the state hopes to communicate to emigrant Salvadorans that they matter, that they remain citizens, and that they still belong to El Salvador. Further, they want to convince emigrant Salvadorans to keep sending monies back home; reinforcing their sense of belonging to El Salvador may be what persuades and promotes their continued financial support of El Salvador.

Recognizing that there are now second-generation and possibly even third-generation Salvadorans in the United States who can represent the future for transnational economic, political, and social ties, a project was developed to specifically target the children of emigrants.[3] Conocer tu País (Get to Know Your Country) is a program that was piloted in the summer of 2000 with a group of eighty students aged twelve to sixteen from Los Angeles, California. The youth had never visited El Salvador. Through this summer program they spent twenty-two days in El Salvador actively participating in a range of educational, cultural, and tourism-related activities. There were also classes in conversational Spanish. The youth learned about national government through visits to the Legislature, Assembly, Supreme Court of Justice, and the Presidential Residence. Natural sites of wonder such as volcanoes, beaches, and national parks were toured. Most important, the youth learned about their "cultural roots and identity."

Beginning with a visit to the archaeological site of San Andres, lessons in pre-Columbian history were accompanied by a ritual performed by a Maya *sacerdote* (religious practitioner). Efforts were made for youth to understand links between El Salvador and the Ruta Maya (Maya Route)—the name of a regional program to promote tourism. The students were encouraged to make connections between the cultural history of El Salvador and the broader Central American region. "We would like to impress upon these youth that their ancient ancestors [the Maya] were a great people, an advanced civilization" (Mario Roger Hernandez, pers. comm., May 2000). In chapter 2 I explored how "Mayaness" has become an umbrella reference used by the state to link archaeology not only to national identity but to tourism; and in chapter 3 I described how it is also used by indigenous organizations and people who emphasize historical and contemporary connections to Maya groups in the region. Still, that this government program emphasized Maya in lieu of Nahuat or Lenca cultural histories can also be interpreted as marginalizing contemporary indigenous populations and barring them from self-representation of their culture and identity. When I asked whether the youth had the chance to visit any contemporary indigenous communities, Dr. Hernandez gave me the same glance so many officials have shown during my years of research whenever I have tried to pinpoint government attitude and policy toward contemporary indigenous populations. It was a skeptical expression followed by a wall of silence. I followed up with something that I knew to be true. "It's just that there are Salvadorans who live in California who are interested in discovering their indigenous heritage by connecting with contemporary communities." More silence. Beyond the experience of a Maya sacerdote conducting an ancient ritual, the program designed for visiting youth would not orient them to learning about El Salvador's contemporary indigenous populations. A visit to Suchitoto educated the youth about colonial history. And to learn about contemporary Salvadoran culture, the youth met with a variety of national artists. They also met with local Salvadoran youth of their same age.

Another creative attempt by Dr. Hernandez's office was to recognize the artistic talents of Salvadorans in the diaspora. In 2000 the First International Painting Competition (Primero Concurso Internacional de Pintura) was held as "homage to the Salvadoran Community in the exterior." The competition permitted only works of art by Salvadoran emigrants. Judges selected five winning paintings. The images became commemorative postage stamps for El Salvador. Because postage stamps circulate nationally and internationally, they serve many functions. The special stamps acknowledge the value and contribution of Salvadorans in the diaspora. They communicate the inclusion of faraway Salvadorans as members of the nation-state. Thus they are tools for strengthening the ties and collective identity of faraway Salvadorans. The commemorative postage stamps are one small example of how the state extends its reach and attempts to remake the meaning of national belonging by drawing positive attention to Salvadorans who live abroad. Rather than restrict the definition of El Salvador to populations living within the territorial boundaries of the nation-state, a twenty-first-century definition includes faraway transnational citizens as well as their present and future progeny.

Media Alliances, Departamento 15, and the Remapping of El Salvador

Throughout this book I examine how popular media projects facilitate and are in alignment with state-led nation-building practices. While the state was strengthening ties between Salvadoran emigrants and the nation-state, the national media played an important supporting role. Benedict Anderson ([1983] 2006) described the historical emergence of print media (which he refers to as print capitalism) for producing and circulating messages in the vernacular language about the nation, a process essential to the formation of independent nation-states. Anderson's thesis has been criticized by scholars who demonstrate how print media also worked against hegemonic projects of nation-building. That said, the ability to circulate information over a wide territory helped to create communities of interest and generated shared meanings among people who would likely never meet face to face. Nation-state interests were served in the process. Contemporary media in El Salvador indeed served postwar nation-building interests. As mentioned in chapter 1, television has emerged as a major source of media for Salvadorans. In addition, newspapers (in both print and online electronic formats) provide Salvadorans a fundamental source of ideas about national history, culture, and identity. My research noted how editorial-opinion submissions and letters to the editor combine with news stories and special features to communicate and also debate the meaning of national belonging. Daily newspapers, therefore, offer an important forum for the promotion of official and other ideas about the nation. They are an invaluable resource for research on nation-building practices.

One important media project demonstrates the creative role of print media to reach out to faraway citizens and to raise national awareness about emigration and diasporic Salvadorans. On April 3, 2000, *La Prensa Gráfica*, one of El Salvador's major daily newspapers, created a forum to link the daily lives of faraway Salvadorans to everyday people and events in El Salvador. Under its national news section there appeared a new column: *Departamento 15*. What and where is *Departamento 15*? El Salvador is geographically and administratively composed of fourteen departments under which municipal governments are structured. *Departamento 15* adds to a conventional definition of national territory. The concept represents an imaginary space and refers to wherever in the world the estimated two million Salvadoran emigrants reside. This innovative remapping of national territory responds to the impact and influence of out-migration on Salvadoran state and society. For sojourners who wish to remain connected to El Salvador, *Departamento 15* acknowledges they have a place within a newly reimagined postwar nation.

On the first day that *Departamento 15* appeared in *La Prensa Gráfica*, the editors stated the following goals:

- to share the histories of Salvadorans who have excelled in other countries;
- to present the entrepreneurial initiatives that this cultural exchange has promoted;
- to divulge the experiences of Salvadorans in distinct fields of culture, sports, science, and technology; and
- to give importance to the effect that migrations have had on our culture and our local development. (Translation mine.)

There is an obvious emphasis on recognizing the accomplishments of successful Salvadorans abroad. There is a link to the state-led Competitivity Program that also seeks to identify successful Salvadorans throughout the world and to build networks and partnerships with them. Showcasing individuals with "success" stories will more likely facilitate the desired creation of international business networks, expanded social contacts, and the formation of bridges between international institutions of higher education. However, it is hard to imagine that the toil of dishwashers, housecleaners, or other low-end workers will ever be featured in the column.

Additionally, *Departamento 15* offers a space for any emigrant to post online messages to lament their estrangement from El Salvador. On June 22, 2000, the column's subheading was "To miss my country is . . ." (Extrañar a mi pais es . . .). Salvadorans abroad were asked to e-mail their response to the prompt and to share their thoughts and feelings with all of El Salvador. I monitored the online postings for months. They included detailed recollections and nostalgia for: "my mother's cooking," "futbol (soccer) on the weekends," "Pupuseria Margoth" (a popular family-style restaurant); and "Puerto Libertad" (seaside sojourn). Some offered individualized greetings to particular loved ones from afar. Today *Departamento 15* is a well-developed section of *La Prensa Gráfica*'s online website. "To miss my country . . ." is no longer a feature, though under the link "social service" (*servicio social*), Salvadorans both "here and there" post announcements that typically involve efforts to locate a particular family member who has fallen out of contact. This and other innovative media forums bring Salvadoran emigrants into the national imagination. They allow Salvadorans in the diaspora to share their longing for a beloved homeland and help to establish long-distance ties with the nation-state. They offer an example of how the media join state efforts to incorporate Salvadoran emigrants into the national sphere and help to reshape the meaning of national belonging in the twenty-first century.

Long Distance Political Participation

The state has certain aspirations for the participation of long-distance citizens. These goals are linked primarily to advancing economic projects, whether by partnering with emigrants or directing the activities of hometown associations, or by forming and expanding social and economic networks through successful individuals.

Diasporic Salvadorans, invited to participate in the nation from afar, also opt for political involvement. Scholars explore the political dimensions of Salvadoran transnationalism and understand that the dialectics of new forms of long-distance citizenship shape the meaning of national belonging in the twenty-first century. Patricia Landolt (2008) includes hometown associations as one among many ways that Salvadorans engage in transnational politics. In addition to the village-level transnational practices of hometown associations that typically focus on local and personal ties, she references the political practices that connect members of the Salvadoran diaspora at the national political level, including oppositional politics. Beyond the level of household or hometown associations there exist well-developed lobbying and solidarity networks. Networks established to provide support during the tumultuous civil war have evolved to represent the rights of Salvadoran migrants and to aid long-distance national participation for faraway citizens. In recent scholarship, Arpi Miller (2011) examines the link between civil war solidarity activism and the contemporary work of the Salvadoran American National Association; Héctor Perla, Jr. (2010) reports on the influence of transnational grassroots activism to the election of FMLN presidential candidate Mauricio Funes in 2009; and Cecilia M. Rivas (2010) discusses how the media and online forums are sites where Salvadorans and emigrants debate the possibility of emigrants voting in El Salvador's national elections. Reflecting the fast pace of change, and following the decision of other nation-states to respond to the new demands of transnational belonging, on June 1, 2011, President Mauricio Funes announced that beginning in 2014 Salvadorans living outside of national territory will have the right to vote in national elections. The UN Development Program will aid the government of El Salvador to formulate the particular requirements and procedures of the new proposal.

The 2004 presidential election provided an earlier demonstration of emigrants' new importance to politics in El Salvador. The contest became a close race between conservative party candidate, Tony Saca, and leftist candidate Sharfik Handal. In the weeks leading up to the election, media in El Salvador and in the United States focused on the involvement of some Salvadoran emigrants, describing them as active long-distance campaigners and fundraisers for their favored candidates. Some who were interviewed indicated they would return to El Salvador to cast a vote.

Beyond their long-distance participation, the presidential contest revealed another dimension of the political value of emigrants. Fearing defeat, the incumbent ARENA party began to link the election outcomes to the fate of Salvadorans in the United States. If the FMLN were to win, an outcome deemed unfavorable to the US government, there would be an immediate backlash and Salvadorans without permanent residency or citizenship would be forced to leave the United States. Fear mongering exacerbated fear and anxiety about the election. As a reminder of Cold War–era, anti-communist political commitments, US government officials, including Assistant Secretary of State Roger Noriega and White House Special Assistant Otto Reich, hinted that such a US government reaction was possible (Rubin 2004). Televised political ads in El Salvador warned that a vote for Handal would risk the flow of remittances from Salvadorans in the United States. The ads claimed that by invoking the ire of the United States, the vote would jeopardize the status of family members and friends living abroad. The strategy of fear mongering discredited the FMLN by placing the well-being of faraway Salvadorans into the center of the national presidential election and regional geopolitics.

Tony Saca won the election with 58 percent of the vote and Schafik Handal trailed with 36 percent of votes. In the post-election analyses, some blamed the FMLN for choosing a hard-liner as a candidate. Others pointed to US interference and the scare tactics of ARENA. Regardless of the outcome, the election highlighted the new role of faraway Salvadorans, including their multidimensional political capital. The 2009 presidential elections proved to be another close race between ARENA and FMLN candidates. This time there was public pressure on the US government to publicly state that they would not interfere, and that they would support whichever candidate prevailed. The 2009 election results were historic, and the victory of Mauricio Funes and the FMLN party provided the political Left its first opportunity to govern the nation after decades of conservative rule. When President Barack Obama visited El Salvador in March 2011 during a brief Latin American tour that also included Brazil and Chile, many on the Left pointed to the visit as evidence that the

United States now has a different relationship with the Left in the Salvadoran diaspora and within El Salvador.

Migration, Transnationalism, and the Discontented

Most of the attention to emigration and to the opportunities for long-distance transnational participation of faraway citizens described thus far accents the perceived positive influences and results of migration. There are darker, less-positive side effects that also influence postwar El Salvador. Some children are left behind while their parents emigrate in an effort to ensure their families a better future. The fragmentation of families is thought to contribute to social disorder, especially when children feel abandoned or reject being raised by elders or other nonparent family members. Further, as criminalized Salvadorans are deported from the United States back to El Salvador, the influence of gang culture and violent and criminal activity has grown. These circumstances point to the challenges of a nation-state that today relies on migration for survival.

There is no systematic study of how many youth are left behind when parents migrate to the north, in large part because it is the undocumented migrant who may be desperately forced to forsake his or her children in a quest to secure economic survival. Anecdotal and individual case studies often appear in national popular media. Many parents intend to send for their children once they become established in the new homeland, typically the United States. These are families with extremely limited resources, and despite efforts at long-distance parenting facilitated by cell phones, videos, and the ability to easily transfer money, separation can be devastating to the younger generation. In ideal cases, youth are left in the care of one adult parent. In other cases media report that youth are left in the care of grandparents or older siblings, or left in a situation where they must virtually care for themselves. Some young children attempt to venture on their own to the United States. Journalists and filmmakers have captured this heartbreaking aspect of contemporary migration.[4] It is a dangerous journey, with no guarantee of family reunification or of restoring the emotional ties that once existed but that distance and time often erode.

In El Salvador entire families are now becoming dependent on the monthly remittances sent by faraway citizens. While the government understands the need for such contributions and appreciates the economic donations, it is also common for government officials to scorn those who rely solely on the money of faraway others. The biggest criticism is that the reliance on remittances diminishes the drive for them to be productive citizens at home. Further, many who receive remittances from family abroad await their opportunity to also emigrate and be reunited with faraway loved ones. For many in El Salvador, then, the phenomenon of out-migration has created a view of the future that involves engaging with loved ones who do not live in El Salvador, as well as the prospect that those in El Salvador will one day leave El Salvador as well. Salvadoran writer Miguel Huezo Mixco (2009) depicts Salvadorans as having "one foot here and another over there" (un pie aquí y otra allá).

Another grave concern of state and society alike involves the repatriation of certain criminalized Salvadorans from the United States. In particular, the return of gang members has influenced the growth and spread of gang activity in El Salvador. The phenomenon is also affecting Mexico and other Central American countries. The judicial circumstances that force the return of criminalized individuals to El Salvador, regardless of whether they arrived to the United States as minors, regardless of whether or not they speak Spanish, and regardless of whether or not they have family contacts in El Salvador, demonstrate a complexity of transnationalism. These individuals usually arrived in the United States from El Salvador as children. Once in the United States, factors of race, ethnicity, poverty, and the lack of citizenship contribute to the shaping of a marginal existence. In the 1980s these factors resulted in the growth of new urban gangs. Gangs such as the notorious Mara Salvatrucha MS 13, based on membership of Salvadoran and other Central American origins, emerged in Los Angeles to protect against existing Mexican-American and African-American gangs. They offered street authority and community protection in exchange for loyalty and compliance with countercultural norms, including illegality. Today the Mara Salvatrucha is a formidable criminal network that extends into the Americas and into Europe as well. The increasingly tough criminal justice laws in the United States punish noncitizen offenders by deporting them to their country of origin. Consequently El Salvador is receiving its share of deportees.

When deported gang members first began to arrive in the late 1990s, with their fine-tuned swaggers, saggy baggy jeans, multiple tattoos, looping chains, and other dangling accoutrement, they confronted social realities that were worlds apart from their mostly urban US experiences. Today in El Salvador, homegrown gangs have emerged, influenced by the gang culture practiced by deportees and probably from popular culture as well. From their complete tattooing of faces, to the infrequent but nonetheless ghoulish beheading of victims, the gangs in El Salvador are an extreme expression of their US counterparts. Undoubtedly the experience of civil war atrocities, including death squads, massacres, and paramilitary violence, informs El Salvador's terrifying gang culture of violence. Yet the blame tends to be placed foremost on the gangs from the United States and on the repatriated.

In 2004 the government of El Salvador estimated that there were 30,000 gang members in El Salvador.[5] In 2003 the government passed its first anti-gang legislation, referred to as Plan Mano Dura (Plan Iron Fist). Criticized for violating civil rights, the new law permitted the arrest of individuals suspected of being gang members and imposed a two- to three-year imprisonment for mere association with a gang. If a weapon was found during arrest, an additional six years could be applied to their prison term. The courts grappled with the constitutionality of the legislation. This resulted in a revised law renamed Plan Super Mano Dura (Plan Super Iron Fist). This version was also criticized because it allowed for individuals to be arrested for merely appearing to be a gang member, and because the military was called to patrol the streets to aid in the search and arrest. To many, this harked back to the authoritarianism that motivated the civil war. It was not a response suited for a nation transitioning from war to peace and from authoritarianism to participatory democracy.

To counter the criticism, in 2004 newly elected president Tony Saca introduced gang rehabilitation programs such as Plan Mano Amiga (Plan Helping Hand). Though the government claimed the program's success, pointing to the arrest of seventy gang leaders and the creation of a national database with information about known gang members, the overall problem of gang violence, extortion, and criminality did not abate. A Washington Office on Latin America (WOLA) report on the topic states that despite the government's zero-tolerance strategy, "homicides increased every single year from 39 per 100,000 in 2003 to 72 per 100,000 in 2009" (WOLA 2011). The report also indicates that during this period gangs transformed from neighborhood-based to more regionally and nationally linked gangs, and into groups that structured for organized, economically motivated crimes. The strict anti-gang legislation negatively impacted El Salvador's police force. There was frequent police abuse and a climate of tolerance of their extrajudicial activities—characteristics that contradicted postwar efforts to replace military with national civilian police while also attempting to institutionalize an effective judicial system.

Since taking office in 2009, the administration of President Mauricio Funes is attempting a different strategy to tackle crime and violence. Instead of the "mano duro" approaches of the past, the new approach will emphasize community-based approaches to tackling crime, coupled with greater attention to the professionalizing of El Salvador's law enforcement institutions. For example, recent efforts to reassert control over prisons include using signal blocking equipment to prevent prisoners from using cell phones to make calls for engaging in illicit activity. These new measures may be having an effect; in 2010 both homicide and extortion rates dropped. Although the homicide rate dropped from thirteen a day to eleven a day, it is still extremely high. It remains to be seen if new policies will have the desired effect: to bring down crime and violence. When considering solutions, the dark side effects of migration and transnationalism must be considered as part and parcel of the dynamics that contribute to crime and insecurity in postwar El Salvador, demonstrating their influence on twenty-first-century national belonging.

As this chapter illustrates, out-migration and diaspora are conditions that fundamentally influence contemporary El Salvador, reshaping the meaning of national belonging. State-led practices communicate appreciation for the financial support of faraway citizens, but seek greater ways to be involved with the investments.

Migration and long-distance participation of faraway citizens reconfigure the economic, political, and social spheres in El Salvador. The constant movement of bodies exiting and returning to the nation also involves an ebb and flow of cultural forces that accompany the dynamics of migration and transnational practices.

Government officials in El Salvador theorize that to keep remittance levels strong, faraway citizens need an affective bond of loyalty, or sense of belonging to the nation. Therefore, the state directs the nation-building efforts it applies at home to faraway citizens as well. State-led projects supported by popular media efforts reach out to diasporic Salvadorans and provide them with certain postwar promotions of culture, history, and identity. Even as state-led projects at home involve simultaneous approaches to the question of national culture and identity, ranging from universal values to indigenous roots, deterritorialized state practices reach out to faraway Salvadorans and encourage them to consider what makes them uniquely Salvadoran, what binds them eternally to El Salvador.

Among the important sites that shape a shared meaning of national belonging are national museums and monuments. Through exhibition and public rituals, these sites stir thoughts and emotions about the nation. The next chapter examines the new national Museum of Anthropology and how it represents the postwar nation. It also explores the emergence of other public museums and monuments that both reinforce and counter official representations and that, in particular, challenge the state to do more to remember, to address the nation's troubled past, and to offer a more inclusive notion of national belonging.

5

Remembering and Belonging

Museums, Monuments, and National Memory Including the Violence of Civil War

A NUMBER OF POSTWAR museums were constructed during the years of my research in El Salvador. They created new forums for presenting and debating, even contesting, ideas about the nation's past, present, and its imaginable future. Some museums were aligned with other simultaneously occurring state-led strategies discussed in this book such as school curricula, history textbooks, popular media projects, and government programs and policies. This is especially true of museums that made indigenous heritage the symbolic basis of a unique national identity. Museums accomplished this primarily by consolidating information and meanings that could also be found at specific archaeological sites, including small archaeological site museums scattered throughout El Salvador. Beyond deep archaeological cultural roots, museum displays also connected El Salvador's distinctiveness through more recent expressions of indigenous culture. One museum notably supported the rights of contemporary indigenous populations. This was in contrast to state projects that presented a homogeneous national population influenced by indigeneity but that did not recognize ethnic and racial minority subpopulations. In addition, both state-led and nonofficial museums focused on faraway and migrating Salvadorans, a segment of the population that has been newly included in postwar definitions of national belonging. With museums functioning as a central site for shaping meanings about the nation, the emphasis on migration and diaspora give further proof that nation-building today is a transnational project. By connecting to themes explored throughout this book and beyond, all of the postwar museums highlighted important aspects of what it means to be from El Salvador.

This chapter considers four postwar museums in San Salvador, the nation's capital, and also two monuments to the civil war, one in the geographic region of Morazan and one in San Salvador. First I focus on the Museo Nacional de Antropología (MUNA), the government's National Museum of Anthropology, and then compare it to the Museo Universitario de Antropología at the Universidad Tecnológica de El Salvador, a privately funded university museum; the Museo de Arte de El Salvador (MARTE), a nonprofit museum and the nation's only art museum; and the Museo de la Palabra y el Imagen (Museum of the Word and the Image), also known as MUPI, owned and operated by a grassroots nonprofit social justice advocacy organization. I explore how these public museums reinforced state strategies in some ways and challenged them in other ways by communicating more inclusive meanings about the nation. As such, nonstate museums preserved national memories that state-led projects to date do not. Finally, I discuss two postwar monuments. First, the Monument to the Memory and the Truth (Monumento a la Memoria y la Verdad) was erected in December 2003 in downtown San Salvador and lists the names of over 250,000 people who were killed or disappeared during the repression of the 1970s and the civil war. Second, the El Mozote Memorial in rural Morazan commemorates the military massacre of an entire rural village. This chapter expands the book's discussion of the dynamic interplay of actors, sites, and practices involved with shaping shared meanings, including shaping social memories, about national belonging in postwar El Salvador.

In chapter 2 I explored "pastness" in the context of new attention to national history, including how the development of new history textbooks and academic programs in history and anthropology became essential for connecting Salvadorans to a unique national history and identity, and why and how archaeological knowledge and symbols were promoted. These dimensions of nation-building can be examined as trope or as ideology, where a distant past becomes a symbol for the modern nation, or as history lessons that provide facts and narratives about the events that led to the present nation. They can also be studied in terms of creating social memory.

If memory is juxtaposed to history, as Pierre Nora (1989) encourages us to do, official versions or symbols of the past become "history" when they lose their emotional appeal, that is, their active ability to inform social memory. The distinction between history and memory can also refer to the gaps between certain official versions of the past (history) and underrepresented understandings of the past (memory). This distinction points to how meanings about the past remain vital despite official silences or when the state contradicts other understandings or experiences of the past. Still, the distinctions can be hard to note when considering a dynamic process, where ideas about the past are not monolithic or immutable, and where silences or forgetting can obscure what we know about the past.

I agree with Susan Crane (2000: 7) who in the introduction to *Museums and Memory* describes museums as sites of history and memory, places "where subjectivities and objectivities collide" (see also Macdonald and Fyfe 1996). As museums deliberately forge memories or seek to prevent the erosion of collective memories, inevitably personal memories and academic interpretations interact. This explains why museums can be such powerful sites for shaping ideas about national belonging. The proliferation of museums in postwar El Salvador involved state and nonstate actors who sought to influence how the nation was understood. Postwar museums began to tackle difficult, even traumatic, events from the nation's past, and museum visitors arrived with their own memories, experiences, and expectations (Macdonald 2003).

By comparing the exhibitions at MUNA, El Salvador's new national museum, to three postwar nonstate museums in San Salvador, I draw attention to ways that museums supported official efforts to represent the postwar nation's past *and* present. Further, I examine how museums as public sites of memory break official silence about

the recent civil war, initiating an important process of national commemoration for the lives that perished and a campaign to not forget
the conflict that brutalized the nation.

I decided to end with a chapter on museums and monuments because they are among the important public sites that represent the
nation and can reveal contests over national inclusion and exclusion.
In addition, they are locations where national memories dwell, are
conjured, and reconjured. By connecting to the historical references
announced through monuments and displayed in museums, citizens
can be incorporated into a constructed past that is constitutive of
the collectivity (Misztal 2003). The nongovernmental museums and
monuments discussed in this chapter draw attention to the contradiction between the state's general postwar support of national history and, for example, its policy to keep silent about the cataclysmic
civil war. In addition, state-led projects that continue to rely on the
symbolism of ancient indigeneity to represent a homogeneous contemporary national society are challenged by at least one museum. In
this chapter I will show how museums, monuments, and memory
are fundamental to the dynamic process of shaping meanings about
national belonging in postwar El Salvador.

Benedict Anderson ([1983] 2006) recognized museums, along
with the census and maps, as primary tools that helped to define
eighteenth- to nineteenth-century nation-states. While these same
eighteenth- to nineteenth-century instruments were at work in postwar El Salvador, the historical context for shaping ideas of national
belonging was quite different. In El Salvador the museum, census,
and maps were utilized in response to both local and global contexts (e.g., where UN interventions in El Salvador extended peacemaking to culture-building; where state efforts to define the nation
by promoting indigenous pasts but ignoring indigenous presence
were challenged by indigenous populations with the support of
international institutions and laws; and where economic neoliberalism contributed to the exodus of citizens and made the nation-
state dependent on the economic support of migrants). The recent
emergence of museums in El Salvador can be understood as globally influenced, in that today every nation-state is expected to have
at least one such site to showcase national culture, history, and identity. Museum projects in El Salvador were attentive to the seemingly

disparate but simultaneously occurring factors that shaped this particular nation from within and without, responding, for example, to why it was important to promote the idea of unique national culture in addition to universally accepted cultural values, the emergence of new expressions of indigeneity, and the impact of migration and transnationalism.

Museums for the Nation

Over the past few decades, scholars have recognized the links between museums, culture, power, and nation-states. These links have helped me think about the functions and effects of museums that emerged in postwar El Salvador. In addition to offering public sites that share a view of the nation that can resonate with other official sites and practices (textbooks, curricula, commemorative symbols, and events), we can consider how museum-going is connected to civilizing practices that produce national subjects, and how visiting public museums has been described as a rite of citizenship (Bennett 1995; Duncan 1991). Because national museums are also understood as political sites, we need to study who and what are included and who and what are excluded from museum narratives and displays.[1] Important for my analysis is the observation that just as museums are important sites for official narratives about the past, they are also utilized for counter representations (Crane 2000). Increasingly, and optimistically, scholars, states, and societies alike consider museums as venues where social inequalities can be addressed and where national societies can possibly work for reconciliation (Sandell 2002).[2] These different views on museums contribute to the understanding of how museums are shaping meanings about postwar El Salvador. I am attentive to a museum's relationship between culture and power, but also to the relationship between museums and memory.

Museo Nacional de Antropología

As emphasized throughout this book, postwar El Salvador saw new investments in promoting national culture and history. Although under-resourced, the state created the first academic programs in history and anthropology and also devoted additional scarce resources to developing a national museum of anthropology. Today MUNA is El Salvador's premier national museum. Built to monumental scale, the warm terra-cotta exterior walls trimmed in sky blue are modern yet evoke a sense of rustic Latin America. Located near the Zona Rosa, San Salvador's tourism center, and across the street from the Feria Internacional, a venue for large-scale events ranging from trade shows to concerts, MUNA is a major site for symbolizing national culture, history, and identity and arguably tries to conjure a new nationalism—a positive sense of being from El Salvador.

The museum was first inaugurated by outgoing president Armando Calderon Sol on May 21, 1999. Scheduling delays prevented the museum from opening in 1999 and motivated a second inauguration on October 9, 2001, by President Francisco Flores. The museum fully opened to the public in late 2001. It replaced the Museo Nacional David Joaquin Guzmán, a modest site that had suffered severe earthquake damage in 1965 and again in 1986. In 1992 the government demolished the Museo Nacional David Joaquin Guzmán and from the rubble of this earlier, unassuming museum arose MUNA.

In 1992 I visited the old museum prior to its razing and the subsequent warehousing of its collection. It is instructive to compare the old exhibition strategies to those of MUNA. The original museum's placement of bold pre-Columbian rock sculpture, such as Maya stelae, Olmec heads, and ancient petroglyphs, was impressive. Ancient painted ceramic vessels were arranged by the different stylistic traditions of Mesoamerica, extending broadly north and south of present-day El Salvador. While ostensibly a national museum, some of the displays in the smaller, earlier museum were organized around broad themes such as the discovery of America and the Central America region. The former museum represented time in a straightforward linear way, starting with pre-Columbian artifacts arranged chronologically by pre-Classical, Classical, and post-Classical periods; followed by history lessons that included the Conquest of Cuscatlán (by Pedro de Alvarado in 1524), Christianization, the founding of San Salvador (1528 and again at a new site in 1807), independence (the first shout in 1811, firmly again in 1814), and the Central American Federation (1823–1859). The separate Ethnography wing addressed themes of popular religiosity, popular art, traditional rural dwellings (including everyday material culture), and handicrafts.

The dominant strategy by which the former museum represented the nation was to emphasize the "traditional" and the "popular." The use of these two terms oversimplified differences in national society. The museum did not define the terms, but displays of the traditional drew from indigenous societies and cultural expression such as folklore, dance, musical instruments, and material culture; and displays of the popular tended to emphasize rural and small-town vernacular such as regional handicrafts and material culture. Prior to the civil war, the discursive and political strategy of nation-building, as evidenced by the older national museum, was not explicitly to identify indigenous or ethnic groups in society except when referencing pre-Columbian or other depictions of the nation's deep past. This symbolic and discursive museum strategy performed a disappearing act as indigenous roots of the region melded into "the national," "the traditional," and "the popular," and as indigenous populations qua indigenous populations or other ethnic or racial minorities were excluded from prevalent narratives of the nation.

While MUNA utilized the older museum's collection, its initial postwar exhibition logic aimed for a more complex depiction of national society, and a more sophisticated examination of social change through time. In various interviews over the years with staff at MUNA, I discussed the importance of representing the nation's past and present. The shared goal of the museum staff was always to spark collective identification with the nation and interest in its brighter future. Dr. Ramon Rivas, a Salvadoran anthropologist who was one of the earliest on the staff and one of the first persons I interviewed in 2000, shared a vision of MUNA as a public space through which Salvadorans might understand that they are "engaged in a process of consolidating a new cultural identity, a process that has been taking place for 500 years" (personal communication 2000).

The three central tensions of postwar nation-building that both my research and early MUNA exhibitions explored were: (1) how to represent the unique and particular nation while also representing a nation-state shaped by a global context and influences; (2) how to consolidate a collective national identity while also recognizing El Salvador's indigenous ethnic minorities; and (3) how to reference massive out-migration that shapes postwar El Salvador, including how to create affective ties with valuable citizens no longer living in national territory. Through the work of anthropologists and the products of anthropological knowledge, MUNA's earliest exhibitions attempted to respond to these tensions as it shaped shared meanings about postwar national belonging. Below I highlight the relevant exhibition strategies.

In August 2000 I was privileged to receive an early walk-through of MUNA with then-director Oscar Batres. The museum was still far from its 2001 official opening, and our tour included viewing empty cabinets and uninstalled shelving and dodging museum staff as they busily completed the exhibition infrastructure. With an area of 2000 square meters, the museum was designed to accommodate large numbers of visitors. There was a separate auditorium and a vast common space for public gatherings. Adjacent to the interior exhibition space was a 700-square-meter rock garden featuring pre-Columbian sculptures amid attractive landscaping. The indoor exhibition space would include five principal themed exhibition rooms: Human Settlements, Agriculture, Religion, Arts and Forms of Communication, and Commercialization.

The five exhibition rooms were designed to focus on separate yet interrelated topics, and visitors were to circulate clockwise through each room to gain a roughly chronological perspective on each theme, which was to begin with its archaeological or historical expression and move temporally around the display material until reaching its contemporary illustration. Outside the Human Settlements room was a life-sized ceramic statue of the pre-Columbian god Xipe Totec.[3] With the temporally circular exhibition logic, Xipe Totec was positioned at the point where deep past meets "the day after tomorrow." Today the impressive sculpture still stands as a timeless warrior in that same location. Human Settlements, the first exhibition room the museum visitor would encounter, traced pre-Hispanic epochs through colonialism and up to the present. "[The room] serves as a mirror for who we are, where we come from, and who we are now. In a general manner, it will show what we have accomplished and what it is we want to do" (Oscar Batres, personal communication 2000).

This room and every room relied on the power of archaeological objects to communicate the deep roots of Salvadoran culture and identity, and through material display reinforced the state's foundational ideology of mestizaje. The ancient objects symbolized cultural inheritance, but it was a deep past that was mobilized, so separate contemporary indigenous populations were not emphasized. The room made reference to migrations from ancient Mexico and to Spanish colonialism. There would be no reference to the historical human settlement of migrants from Africa, Asia, the Middle East, or Europe to El Salvador. As such, the museum visitor would assume a racially and ethnically homogeneous contemporary mestizo nation that is based on indigenous roots and Spanish influences, with no separate contemporary indigenous populations and no other ethnic or racial diversity.

In the final room, Commercialization, which dealt with trade and economies through time, migration was presented as both an ancient and contemporary cultural phenomenon. While there was no reference to modern migrations to El Salvador, the exhibit did recognize contemporary out-migration and made a statement about long-distance economic ties that new migration fostered. It was an acknowledgment that faraway citizens made important contributions to the postwar nation.

The common complaints I heard about MUNA's early exhibitions from anthropologists not connected with MUNA, from certain government employees working in CONCULTURA, and from university academics were that the presentations were too didactic, provided too much information, and lacked visual flair. In 2004 anthropologist Dr. Gregorio Bello Suazo became MUNA's new director. Partly in response to the criticism, he has already changed some of the exhibitions described above. For example, the Arts and Forms of Communication and Commercialization rooms were replaced with the pre-Columbian America room, which provides an expanded hemispheric view of pre-Columbian cultures. This decision certainly allows the museum to showcase one of its strengths: the extensive archaeological collection.

MUNA is an evolving museum and this is important for thinking about the dynamic way that new meanings about the nation can be introduced into the museum. During my visit in July 2009, director Bello Suazo proudly showed me the changes underway in the Religion room. The backgrounds of the display cases were being painted a vibrant red, and the objects inside were being dramatically lit from below. The face-lift transformed what had been an interesting yet visually weak display into an emotional and aesthetically powerful experience. The changes are sure to please the visitors, who tend to be students from all parts of the nation arriving on school field trips and diasporic Salvadorans returning for brief vacations.

Postwar Public Museums and Monuments

Below I discuss three museums in San Salvador that are engaged with shaping the memory of the nation. It is important to state that these museums illustrate the democratic opportunities that exist in postwar El Salvador. Some critics of postwar El Salvador point to the way that global neoliberalism has distorted El Salvador's democracy and debilitated the relationship between state and society (Moodie 2010; Silber 2011; Wade 2003). This is primarily because the state continues to be forced by international pressures and incentives to shrink the size and scope of government services. Further, neoliberal policies have also weakened domestic economic opportunities, and thus continued to motivate out-migration. Neoliberalism's internationally accepted models take precedence over more creative, less market dependent local solutions that could be more effective at resolving El Salvador's endemic poverty and that could communicate the state's commitment to the same. Despite the challenges of postwar nation-building in an age of neoliberalism, it must be acknowledged that free speech opportunities proliferate in El Salvador, in contrast with the authoritarianism of decades past. That postwar museums are tackling difficult topics, including state repression, violence, and the civil war, speaks to the expanding democracy in El Salvador, and in my optimistic view, to the conditions that can strengthen the nation's future.

In addition to the three museums that I discuss below, there are other museums in El Salvador, such as the archaeological site museum at Joya de Cerén and the Museum of the Revolution in Perquin, Morazan. While it would be valuable to survey all of the museums in the nation (which still comprise a relatively small total), I elect to focus on museums in the nation's capital. San Salvador is the most populous city, the center of national government, cultural activity, and popular mass media, and its museums are where students, vacationing diasporic Salvadorans, international visitors, and others converge. This justifies a focus on the proliferation of postwar museums in San Salvador. Below I provide a brief sketch of the particular ways that the three new museums represent national belonging and the memory work that is involved.

Museo Universitario de Antropología

Over the period of my research, Dr. Ramon Rivas left his staff position at MUNA to develop a program of anthropology at the private Universidad Tecnológica de El Salvador (UTEC) in San Salvador. This became the nation's second academic program in anthropology. Rivas also created the university's impressive Museo Universitario de Antropología (MUA), inaugurated in 2006. Located in the vibrant yet chaotic old center of San Salvador, MUA is housed in the UTEC building named after Anastasio Aquino, the Nonualco leader who led an indigenous uprising in western El Salvador from 1832 to 1833 and who remains a popular symbol of rebellion among some of El Salvador's left-leaning intellectuals and political activists, though he remains absent in official representations of the nation (Arias Gómez 1964). Simply starting from the museum's physical setting, many layers of memory were activated. While the square footage of MUA was much smaller than MUNA, the design of exhibitions was elegant and there was a spacious feel. In July 2009 Ramon Rivas gave me a tour of his university museum and I immediately noted similarities with MUNA, such as the emphasis on archaeological objects.

What most caught my attention about MUA was the wing called Migrations (Las Migraciones). Unlike MUNA, whose early display made a nominal link between faraway citizens and the theme of commerce, the MUA exhibition was explicit about the phenomenon of contemporary out-migration. Museum visitors were encouraged to imagine the dangerous land route to the United States, including the perilous riding atop trains, and the shadows and poverty that characterize the migration experience of many Salvadorans. The poignant portrayal of the human suffering of migration contrasted sharply with state-led projects I discussed in detail in chapter 4. Instead of focusing on the peril, state-led references to migration and faraway citizens focused narrowly on the successful remittance-sending migrant who stays connected to El Salvador and who offers the nation-state a myriad of contributions. MUA's exhibition on migration emphasized how Salvadorans maintain their national identity in new lands, as illustrated for example by photos of families at soccer games and at parades wearing El Salvador–themed sportswear and waving Salvadoran flags. This exhibition was unusual for its explicit attention to the contribution of faraway citizens upon whose remittances the nation depends, and for also acknowledging the human rights issues that surround the issue of migration.

Museo de Arte de El Salvador

Ten minutes from MUNA in the same tourism center of San Salvador is the new public museum of art, Museo de Arte de El Salvador (MARTE), a private, nonprofit museum. It is architecturally stunning and an important addition to the cultural life of El Salvador. Inaugurated in 2003, the museum illustrates Salvadoran society's increasing investment in national culture. Though a nongovernment entity, MARTE's publicly displayed and extraordinarily comprehensive collection makes it the de facto national museum of art.

I have visited MARTE on several occasions over the years and found it to be an oasis, especially during particularly grueling days of fieldwork. The museum contains some of the best-known paintings from El Salvador's foremost artists. Seeing them in one museum, thoughtfully arranged by theme and style, will impress any visitor who may be unfamiliar with the high caliber of national artistic production. The primary way that MARTE complements the exhibition strategy of MUNA and other state-led projects is through its display of artwork that valorizes indigenous heritage. Whether through abstract paintings that reference ancient Maya codices, nudes that emphasize native beauty, or the portraits and romanticized images of native women and pastoral life, as exemplified by painter Jose Mejia Vides, MARTE emphasizes the unique indigenous roots of Salvadoran identity.

In one long-standing exhibition, Traces of Identity (Los Trazos de las Identidades), paintings are arranged "historically, maintaining thematic and stylistic relations along the route to tell the history of our people and country reflected in art" (Museo de Arte de El Salvador 2007). Traces of Identity includes works of art from 1968 forward. What caught my attention was how the paintings selected for display were not only romantic visions of indigeneity but also depicted social movements and strife, and the approaching violence of war. Among them was Carlos Cañas's painting *El Sumpul*, an abstraction of a mass of bodies piled atop one another. It recounts and denounces a 1980 military operation at the River Sumpul, when at least 300 civilians (including women and children) were massacred in the region of Chalatenango. By including paintings such as *El Sumpul*, MARTE does more than showcase the legacy and contemporary artistic talent of El Salvador. It also tells the history of the nation, including its darkest hours, serving as both memory keeper and memory maker for the nation.

Museo de la Palabra y el Imagen

The Museo de la Palabra y el Imagen (MUPI) is a nonprofit organization dedicated to "researching, rescuing, preserving, and showing to the public elements of the culture and history of El Salvador."[4] It is an innovative and unusual museum. As its name suggests, the museum collects manuscripts, photographs, audio recordings, film, video, posters, objects, and publications donated by Salvadoran citizens and from citizens around the world. Of the four museums discussed in this chapter, MUPI is explicit in its dedication to memory work, and it has a mission "against the chaos of forgetting" (contra el caos de la desmemoria). That the word "*desmemoria*" was chosen instead of a more familiar "*olvido*" is intriguing. While desmemoria translates into English as "forgetting," the prefix "des" denotes opposition and negation, thus adding more richness to a description of what is happening to collective memory in El Salvador beyond a simple forgetting. The museum reflects a strong liberal political point of view. It celebrates human rights and liberation and disclaims state violence and repression. The museum emerged from revolutionary impulses but has now become part of the mainstream national scene. While it may no longer be a dramatically oppositional force, this does not mean that the museum shies away from difficult topics such as the civil war or the 1932 Matanza. Conversations with scholars about MUPI point to the neoliberal climate where the presentation of national heritage is privatized. Still, its high profile existence in El Salvador is a testament to the democratic transformations that now permit this site's freedom of expression. MUPI is not timid about bringing attention to atrocities and social injustice or commemorating revolutionary imaginaries.

MUPI was founded in the early 1990s in the immediate aftermath of the civil war by a group of citizens led by Carlos Henríquez Consalvi. Consalvi was born in Venezuela, not El Salvador, and is best known for his radio reporting as the voice of "Santiago" on Radio Venceremos (Radio We Will Overcome) during the civil war. His radio work aided the insurgency while representing the enthusiasm of the revolutionary struggle. It is not a surprise, therefore, that the museum's initial focus was to preserve archival imagery and recorded sound about the civil war. It is arguably one of the nation's central repositories for such resources. The goal of MUPI is to keep memories of the civil war from sliding into oblivion. It is as much a commitment to recognizing those who were tortured, disappeared, or perished during the conflict, as it is to recall how a unified people can influence their destiny.

Over the years MUPI has changed its location three times. I have visited each and continue to marvel at the commitment, creativity, and enthusiasm of the museum staff. In July 2009 I became familiar with its newest location and met with Georgina Rivas Hernandez, co-founder of MUPI and director of the historical archives. While the initial focus of MUPI was to collect images, sounds, and memories of the civil war, over the years its collections have expanded considerably. Included among the major collections that Rivas Hernandez oversees and promotes to the public are images about indigenous culture based on the 1986 photographs of Swedish anthropologist Carl V. Harman; the Indigenous Uprising of 1932; the Armed Conflict from 1980 to 1992; personages, with information on notable Salvadorans, including writer/philosopher Alberto Masferrer (1868–1932), poet Claudia Lars (1899–1974), poet/journalist/revolutionary

Roque Dalton (1935–1975), Monseñor Oscar Romero (1917–198), and folklorist and ethnomusicologist María de Baratta (1890–1978), who is recognized for having recorded the cultural expression of El Salvador's indigenous communities; natural phenomena in El Salvador, including volcanoes, earthquakes, tsunami, and floods; notable women such as indigenous leader, social activist, and writer Prudencia Ayala (1885–1936), and teacher and poet Amparo Casamalhuapa (1910–1971). As evidenced from the list above, in addition to attention to the civil war, MUPI also focuses considerable attention on documenting indigenous peoples' issues in El Salvador.

In chapter 3 I discussed how MUPI was a member of a coalition that protested to the UN Committee on the Elimination of Ethnic and Racial Discrimination in favor of El Salvador's indigenous minority population. Through exhibitions and activism, MUPI endeavored to raise public awareness about the historical and present-day struggles of El Salvador's indigenous people. Its most powerful exhibition, "1932," which concerns the infamous state-sanctioned 1932 Slaughter (Matanza) of tens of thousands of indigenous men, women, and children, attempted to disentangle broader "communist-inspired" revolutionary goals and interests from the specific interests of the indigenous people who collectively rebelled against the repressive state. It is widely recognized that the events of 1932 and their aftermath altered the ethnic landscape of El Salvador, as many indigenous people stopped wearing distinctive clothing, speaking their language, or gathering in large numbers in public. MUPI's simple yet compelling visual display about 1932 consists of a number of rifles suspended from the ceiling and pointed at a collection of hanging "blood-stained" *manta* (unbleached white cotton) clothing, the style typically worn at that time by rural indigenous men of western El Salvador. Archival photographs of the victims of 1932, for example, of bodies piled on top of one another in roadside ditches, and newspaper clippings and related documentation completed the display. In addition, Carlos Henríquez Consalvi and MUPI collaborated with historian Jeffrey Gould to produce the 2002 documentary film *Scars of Memory* (*Cicatriz de la Memoria*). In the film's balanced revisiting of a complicated era of El Salvador's past, contemporary indigenous populations and their political movement are acknowledged. MUPI's representation of indigenous people is distinct from that of the other three museums discussed in this chapter. Its goal is not to idealize indigenous cultural heritage for a homogeneous mestizo nation. Nor does it relegate indigenous people and their culture to El Salvador's past. In fact, for MUPI, supporting the rights of indigenous people becomes itself a symbol for human solidarity and defense of all human rights.

Above I describe four postwar museums in San Salvador: the national museum of anthropology and three private, nonprofit, nongovernmental museums. While I argue that all four are involved with postwar nation-building by offering the public sites for exploring questions about national belonging, there are similarities and contrasts to be drawn between the meanings and memories they produce about the nation. All of the museums make reference to indigeneity. However, state-led MUNA emphasizes it as cultural heritage for a homogeneous contemporary nation and uses archaeological objects as the ultimate signifier of the deep roots of El Salvador's indigeneity. MUA and MARTE also utilize archaeology to reference the nation's unique, particular cultural history. MUNA displays historical indigenous cultural expression but does not emphasize contemporary indigenous populations, their social marginalization, or their political struggle to be officially recognized. Neither MUA nor MARTE pay attention to the current struggles of El Salvador's minority population, although some of the artwork displayed in MARTE idealizes or romanticizes historical indigeneity linked to pastoral landscapes and lifeways, and some paintings at MARTE raise general attention to past repression and state violence. MUPI, in contrast, is not concerned with romantic views and instead emphasizes the historical and contemporary struggle of indigenous populations and makes a fundamental connection that the marginalization of indigenous people is the core issue symbolizing state and society inequities. Further, while MUNA focuses on cultural history starting from earliest human settlement in the region, there is no discussion of the nation's traumatic past. It is silent about the violence, suffering, or death toll resulting from Spanish contact and colonialism, genocide, repression, atrocities, war, or poverty. All of the nongovernmental museums challenge this silence, and their exhibitions invoke society to not merely celebrate the nation, but also to recall its dark past. These more honest reflections on the nation and the telling of its history may address historic and ongoing exclusions and in so doing reaffirm the caliber of state and society relations that are needed to address a divided and polarized nation with many pressing problems.

Monument to the Memory and the Truth

Postwar museums offer Salvadorans important public forums for exploring topics that connect to national culture, history, and identity. The physical spaces enable social gatherings where common meanings can be reinforced and discussion and debate may ensue. Museums perform memory work. This is as much about the deliberate representations selected by the museum professionals for display as it is about the visitors' individual and collective recollection and understanding of that past. Public display of difficult topics, such as past repression, strife, violence, and war, break down walls of silence and fend off forgetting and contribute to national memory. A culture of memory is being created through these nation-building projects. As mentioned above, the memories that the museums create about the past overlap with one another but are not singular, nor can they possibly represent the totality of memories that citizens hold about the national experience. However, the appearance of new official and nonofficial public sites along with other official and nonofficial artifacts such as books, curricula, popular media, music, and so forth bring new attention to the importance of national memory in a way that parallels the postwar attention to national culture. Nonstate actors, in particular, seek to create a culture of memory, which I define as a society that values remembering as a requirement for representing shared meanings about the nation, but also as a tool that can help society contend with all degrees of past and present violence and repression by acknowledging social suffering and society's fissures.

This same culture of memory has found material expression in the Monument to the Memory and the Truth. Following the end of the civil war, a UN-convened Truth Commission produced a 1993 report that summarized atrocities and recommended action that could begin to build national unity. Acknowledging that both material and moral reparation would be required, the commission recognized the importance of memory work for national reconciliation. The report listed three actions: (1) the construction of a national monument bearing the names of all the victims of the conflict; (2) recognition of the good name of the victims and of the serious crimes of which they were victims; and (3) the institution of a national holiday in memory of the victims of the conflict (UN Security Council 1993). This international prescription for strengthening postwar El Salvador is another illustration of the global influences on postwar nation-building. Until recently the government of El Salvador had not moved on these recommendations, opting to preserve silence about the civil war atrocities. However, just as nonstate museums emerged to tackle difficult topics that state-led projects would not, civil society actors took it upon themselves to build museums and monuments to the civil victims of state repression and war.

The Monument to the Memory and the Truth was created by the Committee Pro–Monument to the Civil Victims of Human Rights Abuse and was inaugurated in December 2003 in Cuscatlán Park in the capital, San Salvador.[5] Composed of an eighty-five-meter-long black granite wall, the monument contains the names of more than 25,000 civilian victims, innocent children, women, and men who were assassinated or disappeared between 1980 and 1991.[6] The text accompanying the monument reads, "a space for hope, to continue dreaming and to construct a more just, human, and equitable society."[7]

One other poignant monument to wartime violence is at El Mozote in the department of Morazan. In 1981 over 300 civilian men, women, and children of a single rural village were brutally raped, tortured, and massacred by a US-trained military battalion as part of an anti-guerrilla campaign (Binford 1996; Danner 1994). Only one eyewitness, Rufina Amaya, survived to tell the horrific truth. The El Mozote Massacre drew international attention to El Salvador's unbridled state violence and the United States's support of an immoral war. Today there is a memorial at El Mozote. It is another result of civil society initiative, where Salvadorans urge the commemoration of lives lost to state violence and war.

Conclusion

On January 16, 2010, newly elected president Mauricio Funes offered an apology on behalf of the state for the human rights abuses committed during the civil war. It was a historic event that won international attention and praise. In doing so, Funes broke eighteen years of official silence about the civil war. His affirmation that the state was culpable for tremendous human tragedy was an important and overdue gesture of conciliation to the nation, an act toward strengthening the bond between state and society. International media covered the event, reaffirming the global interest in El Salvador and its political transitions, and placing importance on the fact that the nation's leader had apologized for past state violence. While his apology begins to fill a void, the extent to which state policies and practices will continue to advance the memory work deemed essential for national reconciliation remains to be seen.

This chapter examined the role of museums and monuments in postwar nation-building. Offering much more than dispassionate displays of the facts of history, they are powerful tools that shape the memory and subjectivity of national belonging. What is deemed important for a nation to remember can be a political decision. While some pasts may be deemed too painful to handle, commemoration can be healing. As I have discussed, MUNA, a postwar national museum, communicates the state's priorities for narrating the nation's past but also registers its silences. Despite these silences, the museum provides a powerful public civic forum where the nation's past and present is often the topic of discussion in conferences, lectures, and workshops held at MUNA.

A common approach that museums use for narrating El Salvador's cultural history is to emphasize pre-Columbian archaeology and indigenous roots for a mestizo nation. While some efforts reference contemporary indigenous populations, MUNA maintains the same ambivalent stance of official policies that still do not formally recognize a differentiated indigenous ethnic population. By limiting the discussion of national cultural history to indigenous roots, Spanish colonialism, and the resulting nation, museums also maintain the silence found in national history textbooks about the historical and modern migrations that also contribute to the ethnic and racial diversity of contemporary El Salvador.

As noted above, early exhibitions at MUNA did respond to contemporary transnational realities by subtly recognizing the contribution of faraway citizens, thereby aligning with other similar state projects described in chapter 4. MUNA made no reference, however, to their treacherous journeys or to the strife that many migrants experience. Whether discussing indigeneity, migration, or repression and civil war, it was nonstate museums that addressed the silences of the state and that impelled the postwar nation to remember more inclusively. While this communicates the unwillingness of the state to address El Salvador's traumatic past at this time, it does not necessarily imply that official projects will never tackle such difficult issues. Funes's recent apology is evidence that official policies can change. In fact, throughout this book I try to show the dynamic ways that new reflections about the nation appeared and how state-led projects were influenced by a number of nonstate actors. It remains to be seen what will happen as other public sites and practices participate in the shaping of meanings about the nation to challenge official narratives or silences. This will be a focus of my future research. In my optimistic view, however, increasing public interest and attention to the topic of past injustices may help Salvadoran society chart a future where the intolerable is clearly defined and society is united about preventing its reoccurrence.

Conclusion

NATIONAL BELONGING REFERS to present-day recognition, status, and affinity. It is also about certain narratives of the past and how one's experiences and understandings of state and society compare with dominant representations of the nation. By following simultaneously occurring state-led projects in El Salvador between 1994 and 2010, this book traces projects to reimagine national belonging in the aftermath of civil war. The projects included illustrate diverse strategies influenced by the global context of nation-building in the twenty-first century. UN agencies, a growing indigenous peoples' movement supported by international laws and supporters, and the impact of migration and transnational realities all had an effect on state-led approaches to reimagine national belonging.

I conducted many months of ethnographic fieldwork in El Salvador between 1994 and 2010. Having a first-hand view of emerging state-led nation-building projects enabled me to register new official sites and practices and taught me how history textbooks, archaeological sites, popular media projects, maps, museums, and the census were utilized to generate shared understandings about the nation.

State-led endeavors brought new attention to national culture, history, and identity. Projects involved a number of actors in government ministries, schools and universities, popular media, and new museums. The focus on culture took many forms. UNESCO's pilot Culture of Peace Program influenced changes to national curricula that were based on shaping individual values and behaviors for a democratic society. The program had a universal quality and appeared to be transportable from one postcrisis nation-state to another. The lack of attention to local histories and particularities motivated support for other state-led projects that instead highlighted what was original about El Salvador. Attention to the deep history and unique culture of the nation centered on ancient indigenous cultural heritage. While ancient heritage was symbolically central to nation-building, El Salvador's contemporary indigenous ethnic minority Nahuat, Lenca, Cacaopera, and Maya populations (estimated to be 500,000, or slightly less than 10 percent of the national population) struggled against ongoing marginalization. State-led projects ignored today's indigenous populations by promoting an ideology of mestizaje that defined El Salvador as a homogeneous and unitary mestizo nation in which all citizens shared a mix of Indian and Spanish blood and culture. The approach not only excluded contemporary indigenous populations, but also ignored the history and presence of descendants from Africa, the Near East, the Far East, or Western Europe (excluding Spain). By researching El Salvador over a span of time, I was able to demonstrate a dynamic process whereby the government took steps to formally recognize indigenous ethnic minority populations, thus move toward a more inclusive definition of national belonging. In response to massive out-migration that began during the civil war and continues today, postwar nation-building also recognized emigrant and diasporic citizens.

When Mauricio Funes was elected president on June 1, 2009, El Salvador gained their first progressive president in the nation's history. New state practices are already appearing that relate to the reimagining of a nation. As already mentioned, one of Funes's first actions was to create a Secretariat of Culture, demonstrating that approaches to national culture continue to be important to state goals. Further, in 2010 his administration named social inclusion a national priority, signaling the importance of transforming the lives of the most impoverished sectors of the population. A new Secretariat of Social Inclusion was created to coordinate with other state institutions to reduce poverty, discrimination, and inequality faced by women and children, the disabled, the indigenous, and those with different sexual orientations. This focus on social inclusion attempts to address national belonging in ways that incorporate but also go beyond the projects described herein. With social inclusion extending beyond race and ethnicity to also address class, sex, and gender, there will be a more complete representation of El Salvador's national society.[1]

Funes received high marks from national and international media outlets for his willingness to confront the nation's dark past, including acknowledging state violence committed against its citizens during the years leading up to and during the civil war. November 16, 2009, marked the twentieth anniversary of the assassination of Jesuit priests and their co-workers at the Universidad Centroamericana "José Simeón Cañas." Funes publicly asked for pardon in the name of the state and honored the priests with the nation's highest award, calling it "an act of recovering our collective memory." The minister of defense said the army was prepared to ask for forgiveness for the atrocity. In January 2010, on the eighteenth anniversary of the 1992 Peace Accords, President Funes apologized to all victims of crimes committed by security forces, army, and paramilitary organizations, and announced the formation of commissions to study reparations and to search for some seven hundred children who disappeared during the war. On March 24, 2010, on the thirtieth anniversary of the assassination of Archbishop Oscar Romero by a right-wing death squad, the president asked forgiveness for the crime. Many speculate whether the Funes administration will attempt to repeal the 1993 amnesty law that protects perpetrators of violence from both sides of the conflict. Breaking the long-held silence about the civil war may also require addressing the resulting trauma and repairing human rights in El Salvador. All of these official activities expand the national memory work described in chapter 5.

In late spring 2010 I participated in a workshop at the University of California, Santa Barbara, where I shared a draft of this book with a very engaged audience of faculty members, graduate students, and postdoctoral scholars with expertise in a variety of fields, including Black Studies, Sociology, Global Studies, History, and Chicano Studies. Of the many interesting reactions to my research, one question in particular made me pause and reflect: Was I optimistic or not about the nation-building processes I chronicled? Certainly my research did identify a number of negative dynamics that surrounded the nation-building process: global governance and neoliberalism that tried to discipline the nation-state and citizens alike; indigenous ethnic minorities struggling at the margins of national society; hidden ethnic histories and racial hierarchy; how the necessity to outmigrate is now a natural condition of being from El Salvador; and official silences about past state violence and repression. There were also the tensions between local and global dynamics. Still, El Salvador did not slide back into civil war, and political violence is minimal. Political power has changed hands peacefully and democratically, and the country is often held up as an example for peaceful postconflict transitions.

Further, my research demonstrated that the meaning-making that informs collective identity is a dynamic process. Thanks in part to the practices and priorities of the new government, I am optimistic that efforts in El Salvador can respond to the recommendations of the postwar Truth Commission report that inspires the construction of "a more just, human, and equitable society." If state and society are to remedy injustices from the past, honor lives lost, and embrace an inclusive society, the process will require remembering together. It will also require a shared and more inclusive definition of national belonging. My research shows that the process of national memory work and culture building will require the initiative from both state and society, so that the walls of silence that conceal and divide can fall, and that the meaning of national belonging in El Salvador can exemplify humans at their best.

Notes

Introduction

1. Even though UN Development Program statistics from 2007 report 37.2 percent of El Salvador's population lives below the poverty line (available online at http://hdr.undp.org/en/media/HDI_2008_EN_Tables.pdf, accessed November 14, 2010), there are no less than five new major high-end shopping malls in greater San Salvador, including Metrocentro, Metrocentro Sur, La Gran Vía, Las Cascadas, Multiplaza, and Plaza Mundo. Related developments include the expansion of the nation's Europa chain of general stores that now includes the flagship Hiper-Europa locale. Suzanne Kent (2010) analyzes family consumption in San Salvador, making links between desire to consume and transnational migration.

2. Accurate population figures for El Salvador's indigenous ethnic minority do not exist. Most government statistics estimate 1 percent of the population is indigenous, but these numbers have been challenged (see chapter 3). Some scholars, UN agencies, and indigenous organizations working with El Salvador's governmental agencies to assess the status of the minority population suggest that 10 percent is more accurate (Chapin 1989; Gobierno de El Salvador Ministerio de Salud Pública y Asistencia Social et al. 2001). The elusive population numbers point to the complexities of what it means to be indigenous in El Salvador, including the historical and current impediments and disadvantages to claiming indigenous identity.

3. "En nombre de Dios, pues, y en nombre de este sufrido pueblo cuyos lamentos suben hasta el cielo cada día más tumultuosos les suplico, les ruego, les ordeno en nombre de Dios: ¡Cese la repression!" [In the name of God, well, and in the name of those suffering people whose laments each day more tumultuous, rise all the way to heaven. I beseech you, I beg you, I order you in the name of God: stop the repression!] *Historia de El Salvador,* Equipo Maiz, 2005 (translation mine).

4. Throughout the civil conflict, there were different insurgent groups involved. Toward the end of the war, FMLN came to represent the organized insurgency.

5. Mauricio Funes was one of the first people I interviewed in El Salvador for this research project. The interview occurred in 1996 when Funes was a respected journalist and was hosting *Entrevista del Dia*, a daily program that focused sharply on current events with attention to the political arena.

6. While widely considered a canonical text on the topic of nation-building, *Imagined Communities* has its critics. Partha Chatterjee (1993) reminds us that Anderson only addressed the dominant or hegemonic projects of nation-building and overlooked the competing visions of how the nation might be imagined.

7. Prior government attention to cultural patrimony, museums, archaeological sites, and cultural, literary, and artistic production resided with CONCUL-TURA, a subdivision of the Ministry of Education established in 1991 while the peace accords were being formalized. Many of the nation-building processes discussed in this study were carried out through the auspices of CONCULTURA. One of Mauricio Funes's first acts as president of the Republic was to create the Secretariat of Culture. In July 2009 he chose Breny Cuenca, academic historian and intellectual, to be the first secretary of culture. I had the opportunity to greet her days after her appointment. In February 2010 Cuenca was fired from her position in what appears to be an internal political struggle and not a challenge to her competency or qualifications. In March 2010 Héctor Jesús Samour Canán, professor of philosophy and former deacon of the Universidad Centroamericana, was appointed secretary of culture. In February 2012 Samour Canán left the position to become vice-minister of the Ministry of Education and Magdalena Granadino is the current secretary of culture.

Chapter 1

1. Here I intend for "cultural elite" to refer to the small group with more power, privilege, social standing, wealth, and talent who were consulted, hired, or otherwise engaged with state officials about the projects that rely on "culture" as a focus of postwar nation-building.

2. US$1200 million was promised to El Salvador from European and US donors. However, in 1992, the first year of the peace accord, only US$400 million was disbursed. For the remainder of the 1990s the annual aid hovered around $US270 million. For an analysis of the effects of the gap between aid promises and aid disbursements see Astri Suhrke and Julia Buckmaster (2005). While the aid amounts were not optimum, the arriving funds did influence postwar nation-building.

3. The Culture of Peace Program was simultaneously piloted in El Salvador, Mozambique, and Burundi.

4. By 2000 UNESCO had developed the following "manifesto," a code of ethics for the Culture of Peace Program:

I pledge in my daily life, in my family, my work, my community, my country & my region, to:
1. "Respect all life." Respect the life and dignity of each human being without discrimination or prejudice.
2. "Reject violence." Practice active non-violence, rejecting violence in all its forms: physical, sexual, psychological, economical and social, in particular towards the most deprived and vulnerable such as children and adolescents.
3. "Share with others." Share my time and material resources in a spirit of generosity to put an end to exclusion, injustice and political and economic oppression.
4. "Listen to understand." Defend freedom of expression and cultural diversity, giving preference always to dialogue and listening without engaging in fanaticism, defamation and the rejection of others.
5. "Preserve the planet." Promote consumer behavior that is responsible and development practices that respect all forms of life and preserve the balance of nature on the planet.
6. "Rediscover solidarity." Contribute to the development of my community, with the full participation of women and respect for democratic principles, in order to create together new forms of solidarity. (Available online at http://www.unesco.org/bpi/eng/unescopress/99-38e.htm, accessed May 28, 2011.)

5. Ministry of Education, Government of El Salvador (1993: 4).

6. Funding was secured for a project promoting the role of women in society. It was manifested in mid-1994 through a three-week national radio program followed by a longer print campaign that linked the valorization of women in Salvadoran society with building a culture of peace. There was also funding to install a Cultura de Paz office within CONCULTURA (previously the Ministry of Education's sub-Ministry of Culture).

7. While this book focuses primarily on the role of UNESCO's Culture of Peace Program for El Salvador, other supra-national efforts to promote similar values can be connected. For example, in 1998 the Organization of Ibero-American States for Education, Science and Culture (Organizacion de Estados Iberoamericanos Para la Educación, Ciencia y la Cultura—OEI), an organization that parallels UNESCO but with a focus on regional development and integration, held training workshops in El Salvador on "Education in Values" (Educación en Valores) as part of their program on democracy and education. The OEI program dovetailed with MINED's Values Program. In 2007 the OEI signed a cooperation agreement on education with UNESCO creating a framework for mutual presence and participation on specific education-related goals.

The similarities and differences between these two supra-national governing bodies that endeavor to influence national societies is beyond the scope of this research, but would yield interesting results.

8. For the historical link between schools, nations, and nationalism, see Ernest Gellner (1983); Eric J. Hobsbawm (1990); Anthony Smith (1986); and Eugen Weber (1976). For a recent study of how textbooks influenced nationalism in Mexico, Argentina, and Peru, see Matthias vom Hau (2009).

9. Paul Willis (1977) offers a classic study of how schools inform class identities. Schools can also be linked to a number of other social institutions (the family, the church, the economy, etc.) that govern and exert social control; see also, for example, the classic work done by Max Weber (1930). Recent anthropological studies that explore how schools reinforce citizenship include Véronique Bénéï (2005, 2008) and Kathleen Hall (2002).

10. In 2000, my son Sebastian, then nine years old, was assigned to address his school community on the value of *bondad* (generosity).

11. For specific examples of these and other relevant anthropological approaches to the study of media see Faye D. Ginsburg, Lila Abu-Lughod, and Brian Larkin (2002); William Mazzarella (2004); and Mark Peterson (2003).

12. Scholarship on the role of media and society in postwar El Salvador has examined topics such as sensationalism of violence (Moodie 2009), globalization and the concentration of media ownership (Proceso 2000), and how social movements and politics influence media (ECA 2003; Kowalchuk 2010).

13. Círculo Literario Xibalbá was a circle of writers formed in the 1980s during the civil conflict. The group is renowned in the literary history of El Salvador.

14. The October 20, 2009, report from the UN Development Program names El Salvador (along with neighboring Guatemala and Honduras) as having the highest level of nonpolitical violence worldwide. Available at http://content. undp.org/go/newsroom/2009/october/amrica-central-el-respeto-al-estado-de-derecho-es-el-remedio-ms-eficaz-contra-la-violencia-.en, accessed November 1, 2009.

15. I give special thanks to Claudine Michel for discussing this topic with me and for the useful comparison of her research in Haiti.

16. For other classic examples, see Norbert Elias (1978), who writes about the embodied "civilizing processes" that have historically shaped European table manners; or Max Weber's (1930) linking of the values and practices of religious ideology to capitalism.

17. The concept of governmentality was first developed by Michel Foucault to refer to the "art of government" (Burchell, Gordon, and Miller 1991). Tony Bennett (2003), examining governmentality's link between culture, government, and the social makes two relevant points. First, governmentality extends beyond state power to "a broader sphere of practices where particular forms of knowledge and authority are invoked" and involves (for example) museum creators, broadcasters, and journalists whose expertise is "subjected to forms of validation and translated into particular technical forms . . . within particular technical

apparatuses" (56). Second, in opposition to practices of contemporary nation-states to homogenize culture, there are indigenous and diasporic identities that exist not only in relation to nation-state practices but due to "different knowledges, traditions, authorities, technologies, and temporal and spatial coordinates" that also influence their identity formation (62). This last point is used by Bennett to illustrate the space of agency and contestation in governmentality's theory of culture and government.

18. Carlos Benjamín Lara Martínez (1999) elaborates on the factors that can influence different understandings of cultural identity: rural versus municipal, socioeconomic status (especially different responses built on the opposition between hegemonic and popular understandings of culture), religious identities (based on the opposition between Catholic culture and Protestant culture), local ethnic identities, indigenous identities, and generation- or age-based differences.

Chapter 2

1. Three excellent studies that examine particular ways that Latin American societies grapple with indigenous and Spanish mixed-race and cultural heritage in the context of contemporary racial hierarchy, multiculturalism, and nation-building include Marisol de la Cadena (2000); Charles Hale (2006); and Karem Roitman (2009).

2. The first Centroamericano Congreso de Historia took place in Honduras in 1992 and was followed every two years by congresses in Guatemala (1994), Costa Rica (1996), and Nicaragua (1998).

3. The work includes the iconic "Poema de Amor," a love letter to the hardworking, creative Salvadoran people, ever struggling to survive.

4. "Necesitamos reconstruir el pasado. El de hace milenios, el de la conquista, el de la colonia, del de nuestra nación moderna y aun el mas reciente. Hay que enriquecer la memoria colectiva. Una nueva consciencia sobre el SER de nuestra nacionalidad require de la perspectiva histórica. Y es ese esfuerzo, modesto pero honesto convertido en texto sobre la HISTORIA DE EL SALVADOR, con el que el Ministerio de Educación, quiere contribuir a consolidar esa nueva conciencia." Cecilia Gallardo de Cano, Minister of Education, Introduction to *Historia de El Salvador* (Tomo I), Government of El Salvador (1994).

5. Relative to the magnitude of anthropological research undertaken in nearby Guatemala and Mexico, El Salvador has received scant attention.

6. During the summer of 1993 I volunteered to be a member of the archaeological team at Joya de Cerén. I was there primarily to observe how the site was being promoted nationally. My role was not a glamorous one. I was essentially a gopher for the needs of the team. Still the experience gave me a special vantage point for examining the role of archaeology for post–civil war nation-building.

7. Available online at http://www.getty.edu/conservation/field_projects/maya/maya_component1.html, accessed June 1, 2011.

8. "Lo ve como un pasado que aparentemente ensalza, pero sin valorar. Se ve por costumbre o tradición no porque se sepa el valor que guarda, sino como una questión de moda; y se expresan atraves de frases despreciados, y los estudiantes usan gerundios como: ¡vos sos indígena, verdad! Aunque tenga en su aula a alumnus de Panchimalco, el cual es un pueblo que guarda toadavia ciertas tradiciones precolombina y coloniales."

9. The Cuban anthropologist Fernando Ortiz (Ortiz and De Onis 1947) coined the term "*transculturación*" to refer to a multidirectional and endless interactive process between various cultural systems. Though critics in El Salvador use the term primarily to define a process of dominant culture eclipsing the local, Ortiz emphasized a process of mutual interaction between cultures while recognizing unequal power relations.

10. I use the terms "Indian" and "indigenous person or people" interchangeably.

11. In 1930 General Maximiliano Hernandez Martinez instituted race laws that prohibited Blacks from entering the country. This changed during the 1980s, and the law was repealed. It is common for Salvadorans to still insist that the constitution prohibits Blacks from entering the country.

12. Jan Suter offers a rare study that compares Palestinian and Chinese migration to El Salvador. His analysis focuses on the transformation of Palestinians (but not Chinese) from out-group to national in-group by the mid-twentieth century. He acknowledges the methodological problems of conducting research on the topics of Palestinian and Chinese migration and on subsequent individual and group experiences in El Salvador. Among the obstacles he identifies are rare access to archival sources that would provide information on the personal situation of individuals within the immigrant community; the tendency of scholars to treat Palestinian immigrants primarily as economic subjects, not as members of ethnic groups in a nation-state context; and the general notion that Salvadoran society is ethnically and racially uniform and homogeneous. Census figures for 1930 indicated that in the capital, San Salvador, there were 259 Palestinians (155 men and 104 women) (Suter 2002: 40).

13. In the absence of formal scholarship on Jewish migration to El Salvador, the following website on "The Virtual Jewish History Tour of El Salvador" provides some foundational information, available online at http://www.jewishvir tuallibrary.org/jsource/vjw/ElSalvador.html, accessed June 1, 2011.

14. Jan Suter cites various census statistics that use the categories Asiaticos, Palestinos, and Turcos "that in the majority are Palestinian, Syrian, or Lebanese" (que en su mayoría son palestinos, sirios, o lebaneses) (2002: 43).

Chapter 3

1. I use "Indian" and "indigenous person/people" interchangeably. This is a common practice in scholarship about the Americas. Even though "Indian" (or "*Indígena*" in Spanish) is a constructed racial category, its use is prevalent among

indigenous people in North, Central, and South America, although *"Indio"* is derogatory.

2. There is a lack of scholarship on the extent of the colonial presence of Africans in the territory known today as El Salvador. While there is no presence of historic Black communities in El Salvador, some racial mixing of Blacks, Spanish, and Indians is evident with certain members of the population.

3. Historian Erik Ching finds the idea of urban–rural linkages to be unsupported by the historical record (personal communication).

4. Recent scholarship on 1932 includes Erik Ching and Virginia Tilley (1998); Hector Lindo-Fuentes, Erik Ching, and Rafael A. Lara-Martínez, (2007); and Jeffrey L. Gould and Aldo A. Lauria-Santiago (2008). Films include *1932: Cicatriz de la Memoria (Scar of Memory)* (2003) and *Ama: La Memoria del Tiempo (Ama: The Memory of the Time)* (2003).

5. Some elder women in western El Salvador still wear the traditional *refajado* (woven wrapped skirt). Leaders of indigenous political organizations are likely to wear traditional attire, particularly for key public events.

6. A link to El Salvador's May 19, 2005, report to UNCERD is available online at http://www.unhchr.ch/tbs/doc.nsf/0/7898bd847c643f99c12570270039 9b4d/$FILE/G0541904.pdf, accessed June 1, 2011.

7. International Labor Organization Convention (ILO) No. 169 is a legally binding international instrument that deals specifically with the rights of indigenous and tribal peoples. Today twenty countries, including Mexico, Guatemala, Costa Rica, Chile, Argentina, Colombia, Peru, Venezuela, Brazil, Ecuador, and Paraguay have ratified it. Once it ratifies the convention, a country has one year to align legislation, policies, and programs to the convention before it becomes legally binding. Countries that have ratified the convention are subject to supervision by the ILO, and states are encouraged to report regularly on their implementation of the convention and continued compliance.

8. The organizations contributing to the *Shadow Report (Informe Sombra)* include: Institute of Juridical Studies of El Salvador (El Instituto de Estudios Juridicos de El Salvador); Center for the Promotion of Human Rights "Madeleine Lagadec" (El Centro Para la Promoción de los Derechos Humanos "Madeleine Lagadec"); Foundation for the Study and Application of Law (La Fundación para el Estudio y Aplicacación del Derecho); Department of Human Rights of the Salvadoran Lutheran Synod (El Departamento de Derechos Humanos del Sinodo Luterano Salvadoreño), Museum of the Word and the Image (el Museo de la Palabra y la Imagen), and Lutheran World Federation (la Federación Luterana Mundial).

9. Quote from Miguel Huezo Mixco, *El Salvador: El Censo Borra a los Indígenas del Mapa.*

Lo ocurrido con el Censo y los indígenas es más que un error técnico. Ahora ellos son más invisibles . . . menos sujetos de derechos, menos ciudadanos. Nadie quiere magnificar el tamaño de esta población. Los indígenas son una

minoría, pero es precisamente por esa condición que el Estado tiene la oblig-
ación de proteger sus derechos humanos, políticos, económicos y culturales.
No son privilegios, sino derechos. Y no es una obra de caridad, sino una con-
tribución a la democracia y la estabilidad del país. *La Prensa Grafica,* May 28,
2008.

10. Nuestro principal es servir de apoyo a los pueblos, comunidades y orga-
nizaciones indígenas en todos sus manifestaciones en beneficio de la Identidad
Cultural Nacional. Consejo Nacional Para la Cultura y el Arte CONCULTURA
Manual de Organización, Operación, y Funcionamiento de la Unidad de Asuntos Indígenas. San Salvador, September 2008, available online at http://www.con
cultura.gob.sv/manuales/Asuntos%20Indígenas.pdf, accessed January 22, 2010.

11. I asked, Why was a Guatemala Maya shaman leading indigenous ceremonies in El Salvador? Indigenous leaders in El Salvador have explained it this
way: "We have lost so much of our tradition, and our cultural ties to Maya in
Guatemala are historical and strong." One such ceremony that I participated
in was a renewal ceremony in Cacaopera. It was the type of ceremony that is
practiced in many indigenous cultures of the Americas with unique local particularities. I could write another book that focuses on ethnic group dynamics
and indigeneity in postwar El Salvador. It would note that indigenous identity
formation involves a dynamic process of memory and recovery, invention, and
ambiguity. The research of my colleague Brandt Peterson (2006) also addresses
new attention to indigeneity in El Salvador. For example, he has examined how
certain claims of indigenous identity in El Salvador are replacing previous salient
identities. Still another perspective could link the activities in El Salvador to the
pan-Maya cultural movement that is so strong in Guatemala and also influences
the Maya diaspora.

12. For comparative studies, see Guillermo de la Peña (2005), María Elena
García (2005), Nancy Postero (2006), and Jean E. Jackson and Kay B. Warren
(2005).

13. This draws from an excellent analysis of the potential benefits of ILO 169,
available online at http://www.saiic.nativeweb.org/ayn/schulting.html, accessed
June 2, 2011.

Chapter 4

1. A more precise number of Salvadorans living in the United States may be
available following the results of the 2010 US census. Milton Machuca (2010)
provides a thorough review of the academic literature about Salvadorans in the
United States.

2. Orozco and Garcia-Zanello (2009) conducted a survey of Salvadoran
hometown associations in the United States and summarize the following common characteristics: each association focuses their attention on one particular

community in El Salvador; they have well-defined organizational structures involving a board and a few active members, and the board in the United States tends to work with a parallel board in the home community; most groups raise less than $15,000 a year for projects that both fund community development in El Salvador but that also promote Salvadoran culture in the United States. While not the topic of my research, it would be very useful to know more about the politics of the hometown associations considering that Salvadorans in the diaspora are increasingly making demands on the Salvadoran state to offer voting from the exterior, as have other neighboring countries such as Mexico and Honduras.

3. See Andrea Louie's (2004) *Chineseness Across Borders: Renegotiating Chinese Identities in China and the United States* for a parallel case study of US Chinese-Americans engaging in heritage tours in China. She analyzes the experience in terms of the impact on students' personal identities but also makes the connection to state policies to reinforce the concept of "Greater China" that refers to diasporic Chinese and their progeny wherever in the world they reside, and that communicates that they will be welcomed in China.

4. See, for example, *Enrique's Journey: The Story of a Boy's Dangerous Odyssey to Reunite with His Mother* (2006) by Sonia Nazario and based on her Pulitzer Prize–winning series in the *Los Angeles Times*. *Enrique's Journey* is an account of one young boy who travels by land from Honduras through Mexico to the United States; two noteworthy films are the fictional *Sin Nombre* (Fukunaga et al. 2009) and the Oscar-nominated documentary *Which Way Home* (Cammisa and Lavino 2010).

5. A 2008 Washington Office on Latin America (WOLA) Report on Central American Gang-Related Asylum provides some valuable information about gangs in El Salvador. While acknowledging the difficulty of estimating the number of people involved in gangs, the report found an estimate of 15,000 to be a reliable figure (Washington Office on Latin America 2008).

Chapter 5

1. Key scholarship about museums and nations include Sheila Watson, ed. (2007), *Museums and Their Communities* (London and New York: Routledge); Ivan Karp, Corinne A. Kratz, Lynn Szwaja, and Tomás Ybarra-Frausto (2006), *Museum Frictions: Public Cultures/Global Transformations* (Durham, NC: Duke University Press); Ivan Karp, Christine Mullen, and Steven Levine, eds. (1992), *Museums and Communities: The Politics of Public Culture* (Washington, DC: Smithsonian Books); and Ivan Karp and Steven Levine, eds. (1991), *Exhibiting Cultures: The Poetics and Politics of Museum Display* (Washington, DC: Smithsonian Books).

2. See, for example, Annie E. Coombes's (2003), *History after Apartheid: Visual Culture and Public Memory in a Democratic South Africa* for her examination

of the affirmative role of museums in post-apartheid South Africa. Richard Sandell (2002) edited the volume *Museums, Society, Inequality* that examined the museum as having therapeutic potential, as possibly being able to combat racism, sexism, and gender inequalities, and arguing that museums can be a site for inclusion. Amy Lonetree and Amanda Cobb's (2008) edited volume studies the new National Museum of the American Indian in Washington, DC, exploring the possibilities and limitations of this hemisphere-focused museum being able to repair nation-state relations with indigenous populations.

3. Xipe-Totec is a figure represented prominently throughout Mexico. Referred to as the "Flayed Lord," he is interpreted as a sacrificial deity, an agricultural deity, and as the masculine side of the universe for ancient Teotihuacans, Zapotecs, Huastecas, Totononac, Toltecs, and the Aztecs. The presence of the image of Xipe-Totec in El Salvador connects to the early migrations of Toltecs from Central Mexico, who over the centuries developed western El Salvador's unique Nahuat language, culture, and identity.

4. Quote can be found online at http://museo.com.sv/informacion-sobre-el -museo/.

5. Carlos Henríquez Consalvi of MUPI was a member of the committee.

6. The website http://www.memoriayverdad.org/ lists all names inscribed in the monument.

7. "Un espacio para la esperanza, para seguir soñando y construir una sociedad más justa, humana y equitativa."

Conclusion

1. In addition to her role as first lady, Vanda Pignato, the wife of Mauricio Funes, was named the first Secretary of Inclusion.

Works Cited

Abu-Lughod, Lila. 1991. "Writing Against Culture." In *Recapturing Anthropology: Working in the Present*, edited by Richard G. Fox, 137–162. Santa Fe, NM: School of American Research.

Almeida, Paul D. 2008. *Waves of Protest: Popular Struggle in El Salvador, 1925–2005.* Minneapolis: University of Minnesota Press.

Alonso, Ana Maria. 1994. "The Politics of Space, Time, and Substance: State Formation, Nationalism, and Ethnicity." *Annual Review of Anthropology* 23: 379–405.

Anagnost, Ann. 1997. *National Past-times: Narrative Representation and Power in Modern China.* Durham, NC: Duke University Press.

Anderson, Benedict. 2006 [1983]. *Imagined Communities*, new ed. London and New York: Verso.

Anderson, Thomas P. 2001. *Matanza: The 1932 "Slaughter" That Traumatized a Nation, Shaping U.S.–Salvadoran Policy to This Day*, 2nd ed. Willimantic, CT: Curbstone Press.

Arias Gómez, Jorge. 1964. "Anastasio Aquino: Su recuerdo, valoración y presencia." *Revista La Universitaria* 1–2 (enero–junio): 61–112.

———. 1999. *En Memoria de Roque Dalton.* San Salvador: Editorial Memoria.

———. 2004 [1972]. *Farabundo Martí: Esbozo biográfico.* Ciudad Universitaria Rodrigo Facio, Costa Rica: Editorial Universitaria Centroamericana.

Baker-Cristales, Beth. 2004. *Salvadoran Migration to Southern California: Redefining el Hermano Lejano.* Gainesville, FL: University of Florida Press.

Basch, Linda, Nina Glick Schiller, and Cristina Szanton Blanc, eds. 1994. *Nations Unbound: Transnational Projects, Transnational Nation-states, Postcolonial Predicaments and Deterritorialized Nation-States.* Langehorne, PA: Gordon and Breach.

Bénéï, Véronique. 2008. *Schooling Passions: Nation, History, and Language in Contemporary Western India.* Stanford, CA: Stanford University Press.

Bénéï, Véronique, ed. 2005. *Manufacturing Citizenship: Education and Nationalism in Europe, South Asia, and China.* London: Routledge.

Bennett, Tony. 1995. *The Birth of the Museum: History, Theory, Politics.* London: Routledge.

———. 2003. "Culture and Governmentality." In *Foucault, Cultural Studies and Governmentality,* edited by Jack Z. Bratich, Jeremy Packer, and Cameron McCarthy, 47–66. Albany: State University Press of New York.

Binford, Leigh. 1996. *El Mozote Massacre: Anthropology and Human Rights.* Tucson: University of Arizona Press.

Blom Hansen, Thomas, and Finn Stepputat. 2001. *States of Imagination: Ethnographic Explorations of the Postcolonial State.* Durham, NC: Duke University Press.

Boggs, Stanley H. 1943a. Notas sobre las excavaciones en la hacienda San Andrés, Departamento de la Libertad. *Tzunpame* 3(1): 104-126.

———. 1943b. Tazumal en la arqueología salvadoreña. San Salvador: Ministerio de Instrucción Pública, República de El Salvador.

———. 1944. Excavation in central and western El Salvador. *Archaeological Investigations in El Salvador* 9(2): 51–72.

Borneman, John. 1998. *Subversions of International Order: Studies in the Political Anthropology of Culture.* Albany: State University of New York.

Bourdieu, Pierre. 1977. "Symbolic Power." In *Identity and Structure: Issues in the Sociology of Education,* edited by D. Gleeson, 112–119. Translated by Colin Wringe. Driffield, England: Nafferton Books.

Brading, D. A. 1993. *The First America: The Spanish Monarch, Creole Patriots, and the Liberal State, 1492–1867.* Cambridge: Cambridge University Press.

Brettell, Caroline. 2003. *Anthropology and Migration: Essays on Transnationalism, Ethnicity, and Identity.* Lanham, MD: Alta Mira Press.

Browning, David. 1971. *El Salvador: Landscape and Society.* Oxford: Clarendon Press.

———. 1975. *El Salvador: La Tierra y el Hombre.* San Salvador: Ministry of Education, Government of El Salvador.

Bruhns, Karen O. 1976. Investigaciones Arqueologicas en Cihuatán. *Anales del Museo Nacional "David J. Guzman"* 3:75–82. San Salvador, El Salvador.

———. 1980. Cihuatán: an Early Postclassic town of El Salvador. *University of Missouri Monographs in Anthropology.* Columbia, MO: University of Missouri.

Burchell, Graham, Colin Gordon, and Peter Miller, eds. 1991. *The Foucault Effect: Studies in Governmentality with Two Lectures and an Interview with Michel Foucault.* London: Haveshim Wheatsharf.

Cammisa, Rebecca, and James Lavino. 2010. *Which Way Home.* New York. Docudrama.

Cardenal, Rodolfo. 2001. *Enciclopedia de El Salvador.* Barcelona, Spain: Oceano.

Chapin, Mac. 1989. "The 500,000 Invisible Indians of El Salvador." *Cultural Survival Quarterly* 13 (3): 11–16.

———. 1990. *La Población Indígena de El Salvador.* San Salvador: Ministerio de Educación, Dirección de Publicaciones e Impresos, Government of El Salvador.

Chatterjee, Partha. 1993. *The Nation and Its Fragments: Colonial and Postcolonial Histories.* Princeton, NJ: Princeton University Press.

Chavez, Joaquin M. 2004. "An Anatomy of Violence in El Salvador." *NACLA Report on the Americas* 37: 31–37.

Ching, Erik, and Virginia Tilley. 1998. "Indians, the Military and the Rebellion of 1932 in El Salvador." *Journal of Latin American Studies* 30: 121–156.

Coe, William R. 1955. Excavations in El Salvador. *University Museum Bulletin* (Philadelphia) 19(2):14–21.

CONCULTURA, Organización Panamericana de la Salud. Representación en El Salvador. 1999. Pueblos Indígenas, Salud y Calidad de Vida en El Salvador, available online at http://www.ops.org.sv/Archivos/Pueblos_indige nas.pdf, accessed February 20, 2010.

Coombes, Annie E. 2003. *History after Apartheid: Visual Culture and Public Memory in a Democratic South Africa.* Durham, NC: Duke University Press.

Cordova, Carlos B. 2005. *The Salvadoran Americans.* Westport, CT: Greenwood Press.

Coronil, Fernando. 1997. *The Magical State: Nature, Money, and Modernity in Venezuela.* Chicago: University of Chicago Press.

Coronil, Fernando, and Julia Skurski, eds. 2005. *States of Violence.* Ann Arbor: University of Michigan Press.

Coutin, Susan Bibler. 2007. *Nations of Emigrants: Shifting Boundaries of Citizenship in El Salvador and the United States.* Ithaca, NY: Cornell University Press.

———. 2010. "Originary Destinations: Re/membered Communities and Salvadoran Diasporas." *Urban Anthropology and Studies of Cultural Systems and World Economic Development* 39 (1–2): 47–72.

Crane, Susan A., ed. 2000. *Museums and Memory.* Stanford, CA: Stanford University Press.

Cruz, José Miguel. 2007. *Street Gangs in Central America.* San Salvador, El Salvador: UCA Editores.

Cuéllar-Marchelli, Helgi. 2003. "Decentralization and Privatization of Education in El Salvador: Assessing the Experience." *International Journal of Educational Development* 23 (3): 145–166.

Dalton, Roque. (1974) 2001. *Las historias prohibidas del pulgarcito.* México DF: Siglo XXI Editores.

———. (1989) 2010. *El Salvador: Monografía.* Mexico: Ocean Sur.

Danner, Mark. 1994. *The Massacre at El Mozote: A Parable of the Cold War.* New York: Vintage Books.

Das, Veena, and Deborah Poole, eds. 2004. *Anthropology in the Margins of the State.* Santa Fe, NM: School of American Research Press.

de la Cadena, Marisol. 2000. *Indigenous Mestizos: The Politics of Race and Culture in Cuzco, Peru.* Durham, NC: Duke University Press.

de la Peña, Guillermo. 2005. "Social and Cultural Policies Toward Indigenous Peoples: Perspectives from Latin America." *Annual Review of Anthropology* 34: 717–739.

DeLugan, Robin Maria. 1994. *Everything's Coming Up Maya: Archaeology, Tourism, and National Identity in Post War El Salvador.* Senior Thesis. Anthropology Department. University of California, Berkeley.

———. 2008. "Census, Map and Museum (Revisited): Emigration and El Salvador's Postwar Trans-national Imagination." *Identities: Global Studies in Culture and Power* 18: 1–23.

———. (forthcoming). "Commemorating 1932, Transnational Indigeneity, and the Remaking of National Belonging in Post-war El Salvador." *Anthropological Quarterly.*

Duncan, Carol. 1991. "Art Museums and the Ritual of Citizenship." In *Exhibiting Cultures: The Poetics and Politics of Museum Display*, edited by Ivan Karp and Steven D. Lavine, 88–103. Washington, DC: Smithsonian Institution Press.

Earle, Rebecca. 2007. *Return of the Native: Indians and Myth-Making in Spanish America, 1810–1930.* Durham, NC: Duke University Press.

ECA (Estudios Centroamericanos). 2003. "Editorial: Libertad de Expresión y voluntad de verdad." *Estudios Centroamericanos* 643: 347–362.

Elias, Norbert. 1978. *The Civilizing Process.* New York: Urizen Books.

Elsalvador.com. 2010. Funes admite exterminio histórico de indígenas salvadoreños. October 12, available online at http://www.elsalvador.com/mwedh/nota/nota_completa.asp?idCat=8613&idArt=5220826, accessed June 1, 2011.

Equipo Maiz. 2005. *Historia de El Salvador: De Como la Gente Guanaca No Sucumbio Ante los Infames Ultrajes de Espanoles, Criollos, Gringos y Otras Plagas*, 6th ed. San Salvador: Equipo Maiz.

Escalante Arce, Pedro. 1992. *Códice Sonsonate: Crónicas hispánicas.* San Salvador: CONCULTURA; Ministerio de Educacion.

Escobar, Francisco Andrés. 1994. "Turbios Hilos de la Sangre. Una Aproximación al Problema de la Identidad Cultural." In *Cultura y desarrollo en El Salvador*, edited by Stefan Roggenbuck, 126–142. San Salvador: Imprenta Criterio.

Federación Luterana Mundial et al. 2005. Informe Sombra Sobre los 9°, 10°, 11°, 12° y13° Informes Periodicos de la Republica de El Salvador Presentados Ante el Comité Para la Eliminación de la Discriminación Racial CERD. San Salvador, November 30, available online at http://www.lutheranworld.org/What_We_Do/OIAHR/UN_Bodies/CERD68-El_Salvador_Shadow-Report-SP.pdf, accessed November 15, 2009.

Field, Les W. 1994. "Who Are the Indians? Reconceptualizing Indigenous Identity, Resistance, and the Role of Social Science in Latin America." *Latin America Research Review* 29 (3): 237–248.

Foucault, Michel. 1977. *Discipline and Punish: The Birth of the Clinic.* New York: Pantheon Books.

Fowler, William R. 1984. "Late Preclassic Mortuary Patterns and Evidence for Human Sacrifice at Chalchuapa, El Salvador." *American Antiquity* 49 (3): 603–618.

Fowler, William R., and Roberto Gallardo, eds. 2002. *Investigaciones arquelógicas en Ciudad Vieja, El Salvador: La primigenia villa de San Salvador.* San Salvador: Consejo Nacional para la Cultura y el Arte, Ministerio de Educación.

Fukunaga, Cary Joji, Amy Kaufman, Paulina Gaitan, Edgar Flores, Kristyan Ferrer, Tenoch Huerta Mejía, Diana Garcia, et al. 2009. *Sin Nombre.* Universal City, CA: Universal Studios Home Entertainment.

Gamio, Manuel. 1982 (1916). *Forjando Patria.* México: Editorial Porrúa.

García, María Elena. 2005. *Making Indigenous Citizens: Identities, Education, and Multicultural Development in Peru.* Stanford, CA: Stanford University Press.

Garoutte, Eva Marie. 2003. *Real Indians: Identity and the Survival of Native America.* Berkeley: University of California Press.

Gellner, Ernest. 1983. *Nations and Nationalism.* Oxford: Oxford University Press.

Ginsburg, Faye D., Lila Abu-Lughod, and Brian Larkin. 2002. *Media Worlds Anthropology on New Terrain.* Berkeley: University of California Press.

Gledhill, John. 2000. *Power and Its Disguises: Anthropological Perspectives on Politics.* Sterling, VA: Pluto Press.

Gobierno de El Salvador Ministerio de Salud Pública y Asistencia Social (MSPAS), Consejo Coordinador Nacional Indígena Salvadoreño (CCNIS), Organización Panamericana de la Salud (OPS). 2001. Condiciones de Saneamiento Ambiental en las Poblaciones Indígenas de El Salvador. Serie: Pueblos Indígenas, Salud y Condiciones de Vida en El Salvador, N° 2. San Salvador: MSPAS-CCNIS-OPS.

Gould, Jeffrey L., and Aldo A. Lauria-Santiago. 2008. *To Rise in Darkness: Revolution, Repression, and Memory in El Salvador, 1920–1932.* Durham, NC: Duke University Press.

Government of El Salvador. 1994. *Historia de El Salvador, Tomos I and II.* San Salvador: Ministry of Education.

Gudmondson, Lowell, and Héctor Lindo-Fuentes. 1995. *Central America 1821–1871: Liberalism Before Reform.* Tuscaloosa: University of Alabama Press.

Gupta, Akhil, and Aradhana Sharma. 2006. "Globalization and Postcolonial States." *Current Anthropology* 47 (2): 277–307.

Hale, Charles R. 1994. *Resistance and Contradiction: Miskitu Indians and the Nicaraguan State, 1894–1987.* Stanford, CA: Stanford University Press.

———. 2002. "Does Multiculturalism Menace? Governance, Cultural Rights, and the Politics of Identity in Guatemala." *Journal of Latin American Studies* 34: 485–524.

———. 2006. *Más que un Indio: Racial ambivalence and neoliberal multiculturalism in Guatemala.* Santa Fe, New Mexico: School of American Research Press.

Hall, Kathleen. 2002. *Lives in Translation: Sikh Youth as British Citizens.* Philadelphia: University of Pennsylvania Press.

Hayden, Bridget. 2003. *Salvadorans in Costa Rica: Displaced Lives*. Tucson: University of Arizona Press.

Herndon, Julia A., and Rosemary Joyce, eds. 2004. *Mesoamerican Archaeology: Theory and Practice*. Malden, MA: Blackwell.

Herzfeld, Michael. 1986. *Ours Once More: Folklore, Ideology, and the Making of Modern Greece*. New York: Pella.

Hobsbawm, Eric J. 1990. *Nations and Nationalism since 1780: Programme, Myth, Reality*. Cambridge: Cambridge University Press.

Hume, Mo. 2009. *The Politics of Violence: Gender, Conflict, and Community in El Salvador*. Malden, MA: Blackwell.

Ilcan, Suzan, and Lynne Phillips. 2006. "Governing Peace: Global Rationalities of Security and UNESCO's Culture of Peace Campaign." *Anthropologica* 48 (1): 59–71.

Itzigsohn, José. 2000. "Immigration and the Boundaries of Citizenship: The Institutions of Immigrants' Political Transnationalism." *International Migration Review* 34 (4): 1126–1154.

Itzigsohn, José, and Daniela Villacrés. 2008. "Migrant Political Transnationalism and the Practice of Democracy: Dominican External Voting Rights and Salvadoran Home Town Associations." *Ethnic and Racial Studies* 31 (4): 664–686.

Jackson, Jean E., and Kay B. Warren. 2005. "Indigenous Movements in Latin America, 1992–2004." *Annual Review of Anthropology* 34: 549–573.

Joseph, Gilbert M., ed. 1994. *Everyday Forms of State Formation: Revolution and the Negotiation of Rule in Modern Mexico*. Durham, NC: Duke University Press.

Joyce, Rosemary. 2002. Solid Histories for Fragile Nations: Archaeology as Cultural Patrimony. Paper presented at Wenner-Gren Foundation for Anthropological Research Conference. Beyond Ethics: Anthropological Moralities on the Boundaries of the Public and the Professional. March 1–8.

———. 2003. "Archaeology and Nation-building: A View from Central America." In *The Politics of Archaeology and Identity in a Global Context*, edited by Susan Kane, 79–100. Boston, MA: Archaeological Institute of America.

Kane, Susan, ed. 2003. *The Politics of Archaeology and Identity in a Global Context*. Boston, MA: Archaeological Institute of America.

Kent, Suzanne. 2010. "Symbols of Love: Consumption, Transnational Migration, and the Family in San Salvador, El Salvador." *Urban Anthropology* 39 (1–2): 73–108.

Kertzer, David I., and Dominique Arel, eds. 2002. *Census and Identity: The Politics of Race, Ethnicity, and Language in National Censuses*. Cambridge: Cambridge University Press.

Kohl, Philip L., and Clare Fawcett. 1996. *Nationalism, Politics, and the Practice of Archaeology*. Cambridge: Cambridge University Press.

Krohn-Hansen, Christian, and Knut G. Nustad. 2005. *State Formation: Anthropological Perspectives*. London: Pluto.

Lacayo-Parajon, Francisco, Mirta Lourenco, and David Adams. 1996. "The UNESCO Culture of Peace Program in El Salvador: An Initial Report." *International Journal of Peace Studies* 1 (2): 20–33.

Landolt, Patricia. 2008. "The Transnational Geographies of Immigrant Politics: Insights from a Comparative Study of Migrant Grassroots Organizing." *The Sociological Quarterly* 49: 53–77.

Landolt, Patricia, Lilian Autler, and Sonia Baires. 1999. "From Hermano Lejano to Hermano Mayor: The Dialectics of Salvadoran Transnationalism." *Ethnic and Racial Studies* 22 (2): 290–315.

Lara Martínez, Carlos Benjamín. 1999. *La Formación de Valores sobre la Identidad Cultural en el Tercer Ciclo de Tres Escuelas Públicas y Tres Privadas de la Zona Central de El Salvador.* San Salvador: FEPADE.

Lauria-Santiago, Aldo. 1995. "Historical Research and Sources on El Salvador." *Latin American Research Review* 30 (2): 151–176.

——. 1999. *An Agrarian Republic: Commercial Agriculture and the Politics of Peasant Communities in El Salvador, 1823–1914.* Pittsburgh, PA: University of Pittsburgh Press.

Lauria-Santiago, Aldo, and Leigh Binford, eds. 2004. *Landscapes of Struggle: Politics, Society and Community in El Salvador.* Pittsburgh, PA: University of Pittsburgh Press.

Lindo-Fuentes, Héctor. 1990. *Weak Foundations: The Economy of El Salvador in the 19th Century.* Berkeley: University of California Press.

——. 2003. *La Economia de El Salvador en el Siglo XIX.* San Salvador: Dirección de Publicaciones e Impresos.

Lindo-Fuentes, Héctor, Erik Ching, and Rafael Lara-Martínez. 2007. *Remembering a Massacre in El Salvador: The Insurrection of 1932, Roque Dalton, and the Politics of Historical Memory.* Albuquerque: University of New Mexico Press.

Lonetree, Amy, and Amanda Cobb, eds. 2008. *National Museum of the American Indian.* Lincoln: University of Nebraska Press.

Louie, Andrea. 2004. *Chineseness Across Borders: Renegotiating Chinese Identities in China and the United States.* Durham, NC: Duke University Press.

Macdonald, Sharon J. 2003. "Museums, National, Postnational and Transcultural Identities." *Museums and Society* 1 (1): 1–16.

Macdonald, Sharon, and Gordon Fyfe, ed. 1996. *Theorizing Museums: Representing Identity and Diversity in a Changing World.* Oxford: Blackwell.

Machuca, Milton R. 2010. "In Search of Salvadorans in the U.S.: Conceptualizing the Ethnographic Record." *Urban Anthropology* 39 (1–2): 1–45.

McKee, Brian R. 1999. "Household Archaeology and Cultural Formation Processes: Examples from the Cerén Site, El Salvador." In *The Archaeology of Household Activities*, edited by Mary Allison Penelope, 30–42. London: Routledge

Menjivar, Cecilia. 2000. *Fragmented Ties: Salvadoran Immigrant Networks in America.* Berkeley: University of California Press.

Miller, Arpi. 2011. "'Doing' Transnationalism: The Integrative Impact of Salvadoran Cross-Border Activism." *Journal of Ethnic and Migration Studies* 37 (1): 43–60.

Ministry of Education, Government of El Salvador, et al. 1993. *Culture of Peace Programme in El Salvador (Synthesis)*. September, available online from UNESCO at http://unesdoc.unesco.org/images/0009/000964/096428eb .pdf, accessed October 20, 2009.

Misztal, Barbara. 2003. *Theories of Social Remembering*. Maidenhead, Berkshire, England: Open University Press.

Mixco, Miguel Huezo. 2009. *Un pie aquí y otro allá. Los migrantes y la crisis de la identidad salvadoreña*. San Salvador, El Salvador: Centro Cultural de España de El Salvador.

Moodie, Ellen. 2009. "Wretched Bodies, White Marches and the Cuatro Visión Public in El Salvador." *The Journal of Latin American and Caribbean Anthropology* 14 (2): 382–404.

——. 2010. *El Salvador in the Aftermath of Peace: Crime, Uncertainty, and the Transition to Democracy*. Philadelphia: University of Pennsylvania Press.

Museo de Arte de El Salvador. 2007. *Revisiones: Encuentros con el Arte Salvadoreño*, compiled by Jorge Palomo, May 18–April 25. San Salvador, El Salvador: MARTE.

Nazario, Sonia. 2006. *Enrique's Journey*. New York: Random House.

Nietzsche, Friedrich. 1967. *On the Genealogy of Morals*. New York: Vintage.

Nora, Pierre. 1989. "Between Memory and History: Les Lieux de Memoire." In *Memory and Counter-memory*, edited by Natalie Zemon Davis and Randolph Starn. Translated by Marc Rondebush. Reprinted in the special issue of *Representations* 26: 7–25.

Nugent, David, and Joan Vincent, eds. 2004. *A Companion to the Anthropology of Politics*. Malden, MA: Blackwell.

Ong, Aihwa. 1996. "Cultural Citizenship as Subject-Making." *Current Anthropology* 37 (5): 737–762.

——. 2003. *Buddha Is Hiding: Refugees, Citizenship, and the New America*. Berkeley: University of California Press.

Orozco, Manuel, and Eugenia Garcia-Zanello. 2009. "Hometown Associations: Transnationalism, Philanthropy and Development." *Brown Journal of World Affairs* 15 (2): 1–17.

Ortiz, Fernando, and Harriet De Onis. 1947. *Cuban Counterpoint; Tobacco and Sugar*. New York: Knopf.

Paul, Alison, and Sarah Gammage. 2004. Hometown Associations and Development: The Case of El Salvador. Destination D.C. Working Paper Number 3, December. Women's Studies Department, George Washington University, Center for Women and Work, Rutgers, The State University of New Jersey.

Pedersen, David E. 2004. American Value: Migrants, Money and Modernity in El Salvador and the United States. PhD dissertation. Department of Anthropology. University of Michigan.

Perla, Héctor, Jr. 2010. "Monseñor Romero's Resurrection: Transnational Salvadoran Organizing." *NACLA* 43 (6): 25–31.

Peterson, Brandt G. 2006. "Consuming Histories: The Return of the Indian in
Neoliberal El Salvador." *Cultural Dynamics* 18: 163–188.

Peterson, Mark Allen. 2003. *Anthropology and Mass Communication: Media and
Myth in the New Millenium*. Oxford, NY: Berghan.

Postero, Nancy Grey. 2006. *Now We Are Citizens: Indigenous Politics in Postmul-
ticultural Bolivia*. Stanford, CA: Stanford University Press.

Proceso. 2000. Boris Eserski y la propiedad de los medios de difusión. Proceso 930 (December 6). Available online at http://www.uca.edu.sv/publica/
proceso/proc930.html, accessed May 27, 2011.

Renan, Ernst. 1994 (1939 [1882]). "Qu-'est-ce qu'une nation?" In *Nationalism*,
edited by John Hutchinson and Anthony D. Smith, 17. New York: Oxford
University Press.

Rivas, Cecilia Maribel. 2007. Imaginaries of Transnationalism: Media and Cultures of Consumption in El Salvador. PhD dissertation. Department of Anthropology. University of California, San Diego.

———. 2010. "Beyond Borders and Remittances: Discussing Salvadoran Emigrant Voting Rights." *Urban Anthropology* 39 (1–2): 149–174.

Rodriguez, Ana Patricia. 2005. "'Departamento 15': Cultural Narratives of Salvadoran Transnational Migration." *Latino Studies* 3 (1): 19–41.

Roitman, Karem. 2009. *Race, Ethnicity and Power in Ecuador: The Manipulation
of Mestizaje*. Boulder, CO: First Forum Press.

Ronsbo, Henrik. 2004. "'This Is Not Culture!': The Effects of Ethnodiscourse
and Ethnopolitics in El Salvador." In *Landscapes of Struggle: Politics, Society,
and Community in El Salvador*, edited by Aldo Lauria-Santiago and Leigh
Binford, 211–225. Pittsburgh, PA: University of Pittsburgh Press.

Rose, Nikolas. 2000. *The Powers of Freedom*. Cambridge: Cambridge University
Press.

Rubin, Joe. 2004. El Salvador: Payback. Available online at http://www.pbs
.org/frontlineworld/elections/elsalvador/, accessed April 30, 2010.

Salzman, Catherine, and Ryan Salzman. 2009. "The Media in Central America:
Costa Rica, El Salvador, Guatemala, Honduras, Nicaragua, and Panama."
In *The Handbook of Spanish Media*, edited by Alan B. Albarran, 47–62. Lon-
don: Routledge.

Sandell, Richard, ed. 2002. *Museums, Society, Inequality*. London: Routledge.

Scheper-Hughes, Nancy, and Philippe Bourgois, eds. 2004. *Violence in War and
Peace*. Malden, MA: Blackwell.

Schiller, Nina Glick, and Georges Eugene Fouron. 2001. *Georges woke up laugh-
ing: Long-distance Nationalism and the Search for Home*. Durham, NC: Duke
University Press.

Sharma, Aradhana, and Akhil Gupta. 2006. *Anthropology of the State: A Reader*.
Malden, MA: Blackwell.

Sheets, Payson D. 1992. *The Ceren Site: A Prehistoric Village Buried by Volcanic Ash in Central America*. Fort Worth, TX, and Orlando, FL: Harcourt Brace Jovanovich College Publishers.

Sheets, Payson D., ed. 1983. *Archaeology and Volcanism in Central America: The Zapotitan Valley of El Salvador*. Austin: University of Texas Press.

Sheets, Payson D. 1989. Introduction. In *Archaeological Investigations at the Ceren Site, El Salvador: A Preliminary Report*, edited by P. D. Sheets and B. R. McKee. Boulder, CO: Department of Anthropology, University of Colorado–Boulder.

Silber, Irina Carlota. 2011. *Everyday Revolutionaries: Gender, Violence, and Disillusionment in Postwar El Salvador*. New Brunswick, NJ: Rutgers University Press.

Smith, Anthony D. 1986. *The Ethnic Origins of Nations*. Oxford: Blackwell.

Smith, Michael P., and Matt Bakker. 2007. *Citizenship across Borders: The Political Transnationalism of el Migrante*. Ithaca, NY: Cornell University Press.

Smith, Michael P., and Luis Guarnizo. 1998. *Transnationalism from Below*. New Brunswick, NJ: Transaction.

Smith-Nonini, Sandy. 2010. *Healing the Body Politics: El Salvador's Popular Struggle for Health Rights from Civil War to Neoliberal Peace*. New Brunswick, NJ: Rutgers University Press.

Starn, Orin, and Marisol de la Cadena, eds. 2007. *Indigenous Experience Today*. Oxford: Berg.

Steinmetz, George, ed. 1999. *State/Culture: State/Formation after the Cultural Turn*. Ithaca, NY: Cornell University Press.

Suhrke, Astri, and Julia Buckmaster. 2005. "Post-war Aid: Patterns and Purposes." *Development in Practice* 15 (6): 737–746.

Suter, Jan. 2002. "'Pernicious Aliens' and the Mestizo Nation: Ethnicity and the Shaping of Collective Identities in El Salvador before the Second World War." *Human Resources Abstracts* 37 (4): 477–629.

Taylor, Analisa. 2009. *Indigeneity in the Mexican Cultural Imagination: Thresholds of Belonging*. Tucson: University of Arizona Press.

Thurner, Mark. 1997. *From Two Republics to One Divided*. Durham, NC: Duke University Press.

Tilley, Virginia Q. 2005. *Seeing Indians: A Study of Race, Nation, and Power in El Salvador*. Albuquerque: University of New Mexico Press.

Trigger, Bruce. 1996. "Romanticism, Nationalism, and Archaeology." In *Nationalism, Politics, and the Practice of Archaeology*, edited by Philip L. Kohl and Clare Fawcett, 263–279. Cambridge: Cambridge University Press.

Trouillot, Michel-Rolph. 1990. *Haiti, State Against Nation: The Origins and Legacy of Duvalierism*. New York: Monthly Review Press.

———. 2000. "The Anthropology of the State in the Age of Globalization: Close Encounters of the Deceptive Kind." *Current Anthropology* 2 (1): 125–138.

Turcios, Roberto. 1995. *Los Primeros Patriotas*. San Salvador, El Salvador: Ediciones Tendencias.

United Nations Development Program. 2009. Report on Human Development in Central America.

United Nations Security Council. 1993. From Madness to Hope: The 12-year War in El Salvador: Report of the Commission on the Truth for El Salvador, S/25500, 5–8.

Vasconcelos, José. 2007 (1925). *La Raza Cósmica*, 4th ed. Mexico: Editorial Porrúa.

Verdery, Katherine E. 1996. *What Was Socialism and What Comes Next?* Princeton, NJ: Princeton University Press.

Vertovec, Steven. 2009. *Transnationalism*. London: Routledge.

vom Hau, Matthias. 2009. "Unpacking the School: Textbooks, Teachers, and the Construction of Nationhood in Mexico, Argentina, and Peru." *Latin American Research Review* 44 (3): 127–154.

Wade, Christine J. 2003. The Left and Neoliberalism: Postwar Politics in El Salvador. PhD dissertation. Department of Political Science. Boston University.

Wallerstein, Immanuel. 1991. "The Construction of Peoplehood: Racism, Nationalism, Ethnicity." In *Race, Nation, Class: Ambiguous Identities*, edited by Etienne Balibar and Immanuel Wallerstein, 71–85. London: Verso.

Walter, Knut. 1998. *Las Fuerzas Armadas y el acuerdo de paz: Lat transformación necesaria del ejercito*. San Salvador: Fundación Friedrich Ebert.

Washington Office on Latin America. 2008. Central American Gang-Related Asylum: A Resource Guide. May, available online at http://www.wola .org/publications/central_american_gang_related_asylum_guide?down load=Central%20America/past/CA%20Gang-Related%20Asylum.pdf, accessed June 2, 2011.

———. 2011. Stronger Than the Iron Fist: Funes Administration Attempts a Different Approach to Crime and Violence in El Salvador. March 18, available online at http://www.wola.org/commentary/stronger_than_the_iron_ fist_funes_administration_attempts_a_different_approach_to_crime_a, accessed June 2, 2011.

Weber, Eugen. 1976. *Peasants into Frenchmen: The Modernization of Rural France, 1870–1914*. Stanford, CA: Stanford University Press.

Weber, Max. 1930. *The Protestant Ethic and the Spirit of Capitalism*. London: Allen and Unwin.

Williams, Philip J., and Knut Walter. 1997. *Militarization and Demilitarization in El Salvador's Transition to Democracy*. Pittsburgh, PA: University of Pittsburgh Press.

Willis, Paul E. 1977. *Learning to Labor: How Working Class Kids Get Working Class Jobs*. New York: Columbia University Press.

Wilson, Everett Alan. 1970. *The Crisis of National Integration in El Salvador, 1919–1935*. PhD dissertation, Stanford University.

Wood, Elisabeth Jean. 2003. *Insurgent Collective Action and Civil War in El Salvador*. Cambridge: Cambridge University Press.

Yudice, George. 2003. *The Expediency of Culture: Uses of Culture in the Global Era.* Durham, NC: Duke University Press.

Zilberg Elana. 2004. "Fools Banished from the Kingdom: Remapping Geographies of Gang Violence between the Americas (Los Angeles and San Salvador)." *American Quarterly* 56 (3): 759–779.

———. 2007. "Gangster in Guerrilla Face: A Transnational Mirror of Production between the USA and El Salvador." *Anthropological Theory* 7 (1): 37–57.

Index

About the Author

In 2004 Robin Maria DeLugan received her PhD in Anthropology from the University of California, Berkeley. From 2004 to 2006 she was a University of California Presidential Postdoctoral Fellow affiliated with the Ethnic Studies Department at the University of California, Berkeley. In 2006 she joined the new tenth campus of the University of California system located in Merced in the heart of California's central San Joaquin Valley, an ethnically diverse region also known for socioeconomic disparities. One of two founding Anthropology faculty at the new university, she co-designed their Anthropology program. At the University of California, Merced, she is fostering community-engaged research collaborations to benefit the region. She maintains active ties with El Salvador's academic community and community-based indigenous organizations. She has published in a number of academic journals including *American Ethnologist*, *Anthropological Quarterly*, *Identities: Global Studies in Culture and Power*, *Journal of Human Rights*, and *American Indian Quarterly*. Her ongoing research in El Salvador examines how the nation is confronting a history of state-sanctioned violence and exclusion and explores the sites and practices of commemoration. She is comparing the memory work in El Salvador with other case studies, such as contemporary Spain's new attention to the Spanish Civil War (1936–39).

CPSIA information can be obtained at www.ICGtesting.com
Printed in the USA
BVOW02s1911231113

337061BV00001B/3/P